"*How to Love Yourself* is an illuminating look at love—a quality hard to figure out even as we are taught that it makes the world go 'round. The book is wise, useful, and also great fun to read. Lodro, from his long-term Buddhist practice, and Meggan, with her Christian mystic background, offer different ways of viewing love as the force that frees us to truly be ourselves, and be happy."

— **Sharon Salzberg**, author of *Lovingkindness* and *Real Happiness*

"The great thing about Lodro and Meggan writing a book about love is that you get perspectives from both a down-to-earth Buddhist dude, and a hot female mystic—AND!—double the jokes and love stories. The result is a lot of truth and modern wisdom on how to expand your capacity to love—in suffering, in sex, in separation, in spirit, in your very real life that could always be filled with more love."

— **Danielle LaPorte**, *New York Times* best-selling author of *The Desire Map* and *The Fire Starter Sessions*

"I so wish I had read this book when I was 18 and just starting out in the dating world. It would have saved me a lot of trouble and a boatload of Kleenex. Meggan and Lodro are not only totally sane in their approach to relationships, they're also practical and hilarious. This page-turner will most assuredly crack you up, but more importantly, it will ease your path to finding the love of your life, whether that turns out to be someone else or the person staring back at you when you look in the mirror."

— **Kate Northrup**, best-selling author of *Money, A Love Story*

"I am so grateful the universe shifted and brought both Meggan and Lodro together to share this sacred work. Loving yourself is no easy task but it's the most rewarding lesson. *How To Love Yourself (and Sometimes Other People)* is a manual that helps you dive deep into the cave of your own heart so you can become your own beloved. This step-by-step guide helps you crack open the most auspicious part of you so that you can walk safely in love. If you are ready to courageously leap out of fear and into unconditional love, this is the book for you."

— **Kyle Gray**, best-selling author of *Angel Prayers*

"Meggan Watterson and Lodro Rinzler have written a modern-day spiritual 'he said, she said' as they guide us along the path to loving ourselves fiercely, ultimately giving way to loving others and being loved. Intimate, entertaining, provocative, and revealing, *How To Love Yourself (and Sometimes Other People)* is for all seekers of self-love and self-acceptance. Give your heart a gift and immerse yourself in the wisdom and lessons this book has to offer—you just may find love where you least expect it."

— **Nancy Levin**, best-selling author of *Jump . . . And Your Life Will Appear*

"*How To Love Yourself (And Sometimes Other People)* has real modern gems in it, and the down-to-earth and complementary voices of its authors, Meggan and Lodro—both young experts in their own spiritual fields—leave you feeling like they are totally present with you as you read these pages. What really helps us to navigate love is a good conversation with trusted friends, friends who don't judge us, friends who actually know what they are talking about. Meggan and Lodro both show their ability to be those friends, to themselves, to each other, and to us as we read along."

— **Ethan Nichtern**, author of *The Road Home*

"Looking for love? Well, stop. Seriously, the search is over. Meggan and Lodro remind us that love is right here, within. There's nowhere we need to go or some better version of ourself we need to become. *How To Love Yourself* is that slap to the forehead that we all can use. This beautiful gem reminds us that we are love and therefore we don't need to wait for a partner to find love. We can get that party started right now-- and then a partner can swing in and join us on this wild adventure of loving ourselves. No stress. No expectations. Just love."

— **Kris Carr**, *New York Times* best-selling author of *Crazy Sexy Diet* and *Crazy Sexy Kitchen*

HOW TO
L♥VE
YOURSELF
(AND SOMETIMES OTHER PEOPLE)

HOW TO L♥VE YOURSELF

(AND SOMETIMES OTHER PEOPLE)

LODRO RINZLER & MEGGAN WATTERSON

SPIRITUAL ADVICE FOR MODERN RELATIONSHIPS

HAY HOUSE, INC.
Carlsbad, California • New York City
London • Sydney • New Delhi

Published in the United States by: Hay House, Inc.: www.hayhouse.
com® • **Published in Australia by:** Hay House Australia Pty. Ltd.:
www.hayhouse.com.au • **Published in the United Kingdom by:** Hay
House UK, Ltd.: www.hayhouse.co.uk • **Published in India by:** Hay
House Publishers India: www.hayhouse.co.in

Cover design: Michelle Polizzi • *Interior design:* Nick C. Welch

The authors of this book do not dispense medical advice or pre-
scribe the use of any technique as a form of treatment for physical,
emotional, or medical problems without the advice of a physician,
either directly or indirectly. The intent of the authors is only to offer
information of a general nature to help you in your quest for emotional and spiritual well-being. In the event you use any of the information in this book for yourself, the authors and the publisher assume
no responsibility for your actions.

Library of Congress Cataloging-in-Publication Data

Watterson, Meggan.
  How to love yourself (and sometimes other people) : spiritual advice
for modern relationships / Meggan Watterson, Lodro Rinzler. -- 1st
Edition.
     pages cm
  ISBN 978-1-4019-4669-2 (paperback)
  1. Self-acceptance. 2. Interpersonal relations. I. Rinzler, Lodro. II.
Title.
  BF575.S37W38 2015
  204'.4--dc23
                                              2015012437
Tradepaper ISBN: 978-1-4019-4669-2
E-book ISBN: 978-1-4019-4804-7
Audiobook ISBN: 978-1-4019-5742-1

1st edition, September 2015

Printed in the United States of America

THIS BOOK IS FOR ANYONE WHO LONGS FOR LOVE, BUT SUSPECTS THAT LOVE BEGINS AT HOME—WITH YOU AND YOUR OWN HEART.

CONTENTS

INTRODUCTION

MEGGAN & LODRO

Within these pages the two of us share many personal stories about how we have joined our spiritual paths to our romantic ones. Meggan comes from a Christian mystic background while Lodro is a lifelong Buddhist. Meggan emphasizes the Gospel of Mary Magdalene and the voice of the divine feminine while Lodro brings in the story of the Buddha and the teachings of more contemporary Buddhists. The idea of unbridled, unconditional love is prevalent in both these traditions. They each have a lot to teach us in terms of how to open our hearts more fully, initially to ourselves but also to the world around us.

We share teachings from these religious backgrounds alongside meditations, exercises, and basic tips. At the end of each chapter there are suggestions for incorporating the teachings into your life; while we provide a lot of discussion, this is where the real work comes in. We are all for joining spirituality and relationships, but it is not a theoretical path; it is one that we are meant to walk.

We begin the book by exploring what it's like to be single and dating before moving onto long-term relationships and all the tricky aspects of commitment to another human being. We talk about sex. We talk about stability. And then we talk about a natural part of romance: dissolution. We suggest that every aspect of this cycle is natural and we can maintain an open heart through it all. We know that relationships can have epic highs and lows and will discuss what it means to ride that roller coaster. At its core this book is about learning to love yourself and how you are worthy of love—both self-love and the love of others.

Meggan

The women in my spirituality group, the RED-LADIES, were seated in a circle with a lit candle at the center, as always. I won't go into the kind of spirituality group we are right now, but knowing our tagline might help: "Some break bread; REDLADIES break dark chocolate." Our topic that night was divine worth. And as each woman shared her experience of meditating on her sense of worth, I had a revelation. It was one of those slap-to-the-forehead moments.

At the root of our search for love is a glaring need to feel worthy of it.

So many of us rack up huge lists of accomplishments in our pursuit to feel worthy. We get two master's degrees, not just the one. (Ahem, yes. That would be me.) We break our necks, bend over backward, and even betray who we really are or what we really need with the hope that we will then feel a sense of truly being loved. We are misled by the false belief that love is something we must earn. That love is something we must become worthy of once we're "fixed" or "whole." That love is something outside of us.

The most powerful truth my own relationships have allowed me to practice is that I don't deserve love. (Stick with me here.) Love isn't "deserved," as in *If only I would have said the right thing, made the perfect gesture, or found a way to be more, to be good enough, then I would deserve love.* But love isn't like that. We don't become worthy of love someday; we are worthy of love simply because we exist. We only need to remember the truth of our intrinsic worth and then claim it. Love is a gift that comes with being.

No matter how broken you feel, no matter how unworthy, no matter how messy the divorce or how many, love has the power to transform our pain and suffering into a greater capacity to love. There's a way to see each relationship in our lives as an opportunity to hone and refine our own ability to love and be loved. So that no matter what comes our way, heartbreak hotel or a happy Hollywood ending, we move forward with that love we have cultivated. We live into the truth that the broken-open heart holds more light than the closed heart too afraid to break.

LODRO

I was leading a daylong meditation workshop in Boston. After studying Buddhist teachings and talking about how to apply them to our lives, I encouraged the participants of that workshop to write down something they were struggling with and submit it anonymously. We put a dozen slips of paper in a bowl and, one by one, I pulled out these questions and read them aloud for the group to contemplate. And then I came to one that stopped my heart. I'll never forget the first time I saw it:

"My boyfriend has never said he loves me. I feel unworthy of love. What can I do?"

The group that day had many wise teachings to offer in regards to this situation. But the question haunted me for weeks afterward. I was traveling for one of my books— to meditation centers, yoga communities, universities, bookstores, everywhere. And the more I traveled, the more I heard various forms of this sentiment:

"I don't think I'll ever find someone who will love me for me."

"If I can't love myself, how can I expect anyone else to?"

"Why am I single? Am I broken?"

In today's consumer society we are often taught that we are broken. And good news! There's something we can buy or achieve that's external to ourselves that will fix us. Here's the real good news: You don't need anything external to make you more lovable. You are perfect and inherently lovable just as you are. You simply need to discover this. In my tradition, that of Shambhala Buddhism, it is believed we are Buddha. We are awake. We are good. That is the core of who we are. When I read Meggan's first book, *Reveal,* I saw that while she came from a different religious background, she had written about the exact same concept: we can discover the love we need inside ourselves. And if you think you're the exception to the rule and that you're somehow not innately lovable, keep reading.

MEGGAN

Lodro had me at his bow tie. We were in Woodstock, New York, speaking on a panel with Elizabeth Lesser and Gail Straub for the Woodstock Writers Festival in the spring of 2012. Before meeting him I was concerned I would fumble his name; it's the sort of thing I'm apt to do. But the second we met, I felt at ease. We became immediate and effortless friends. The gift bag they gave speakers had a notebook and pen along with other goodies for writers. So during the keynote that first night,

Lodro had the ingenuity to continue our conversation on the blank pages of his notebook. Like teens at the back of a classroom, we scribbled notes that elicited muffled laughs and sideways glances (Lodro recently told me that this is called *smizing*—smiling with the eyes). With the back and forth of our inked banter and all that smizing, we both felt a natural connection that was genuine, disarming, and downright fun.

We might seem an unlikely duo. Lodro is firmly rooted in Shambhala Buddhist practice—which includes a head teacher and community, the whole shebang—whereas I am not tethered to any traditional religious structure or institution. If I had been born male, and if Catholic priests could have sex, marry, and double as tango instructors, then I would have an uncomplicated relationship to the Christian tradition. Or if the day came when the pope was accompanied by a she-pope, and likewise there were priestesses (who were considered as legitimate as priests) who could also have sex, marry (same-sex or otherwise), and double as tango instructors, then, again, I would flaunt my rosary with glee.

As it stands, I'm a spiritual misfit who is devoted to directly connecting to the divine as much as possible and wherever possible—not just before a quiet altar but also in line at Whole Foods or while riding a turbulent flight. In a very human way, I try to embody divine love wherever I am. Unable to be a priest/priestess, I have spent the past two decades studying the divine feminine in the Christian tradition and in other world religions. Sacred, noncanonical texts like the Gospel of Mary Magdalene became my spiritual anchor. I'm a firm believer in the power of the word and the impact that ideas and stories of the divine can have on culture. I've drenched myself in the divine feminine in hopes of creating a more balanced idea of the divine for myself and for the women in my spiritual community. Lodro and I have found that we make an interesting yin and yang. And we have some common ground: I contributed to Sumi Loundon's groundbreaking *Blue Jean Buddha*, the first book of its kind to speak to an emerging generation of Buddhists. I also had some of the most whacked-out and amazing experiences at the Barre Center for Buddhist Studies, where I went for a two-week silent meditation retreat while matriculating at Smith College. The heart of where Lodro and I see eye to eye and where our work intersects is in our very personal and mutual desire to be of service. We each want, ardently, to be fully present, fully human, and fully loving. We feel deeply. We have compassion in spades for ourselves and for others. And we have communities of spiritual seekers who are hungry to feel connected not only to their own truth but also to something far larger than their individual lives.

LODRO

From the moment I arrived at the writers festival I was attracted to Meggan. I didn't know what form that attraction would take, but I immediately wanted to know her more fully. I did indeed take out our shared notebook and begin what has turned into a collaborative writing adventure. The keynote speaker, Philippe Petit, who was presenting his book about knots, rudely interrupted the initial flow of our shared work. He refused to talk about his famous tightrope walking, asking the audience only to talk to him about "knots." Unfortunately, his French accent got in the way, and while trying to write to Meggan I saw the 11-year-old girl arise in her, as she giggled incessantly whenever he mispronounced the word as "nuts." "Now I will show you my favorite nut!" Philippe would declare. "Then after I will show you the nuts that saved my life."

As Meggan sat there giggling I recognized much of myself in her, which surprised me considering our entirely different backgrounds. She speaks well to what's at play in our styles: I have spent a lifetime immersed in Buddhism; she's spent hers in exploration of something untethered to a specific tradition. Yet when I met her I saw a kindred spirit. For the last dozen years I have been contemplating what it means to follow a 2,600-year-old tradition while living in a modern world. She has been doing that work in Christianity and other traditions for much longer. My first book emphasized bridging meditation with the rest of life, including time at the bar. Hers was strikingly familiar in tone and took place a few steps away on the dance floor. I knew that her playfulness, authenticity, and deep knowledge of the religious traditions she studied would be enlightening for me.

The part of the story that she may not know is that I sat down and read *Reveal* the next day. My expectations were low; many of us have picked up a book by someone whose company we enjoy and found it to be complete garbage. Thankfully this experience was quite the opposite. I was shocked. I wasn't shocked that she was so eloquent at expressing the human condition, but instead because I realized we had written the same book. Where I share my heartbreak and stories of spiritual seeking in college, Meggan went through a similar experience even earlier. Where I talk about the Shambhala concept of how we all possess basic goodness, Meggan speaks to how we all possess divine love. Both of our books empower the reader to live a meaningful life, the root of which is based in the idea that it is okay to be who you are (sex, wine, and fun included).

MEGGAN & LODRO

Over the past several months and many glasses of wine, we've found that our spiritual communities have similar pressing desires about relationships. They long for love. They long to feel worthy of love. They long for a relationship with themselves that doesn't exhaust or consume them. They long for a meaningful relationship with someone else. They long for sex. They long for sacred intimacy. They long to find the one. They long to get past the one. They long to feel something more than heartbreak. They long.

And we long right along with them.

Whether we are progressive or conservative, male or female, our ideas and expectations about partnership have shifted because of cultural mores. We are more often seeking an equal, someone who will respect our personal growth. We're not looking to be saved. We've gotten the memo that the white knight is a myth and that the princess has come down from her tower, restless of waiting. We've become our own saviors. We're looking for something that is not often seen. A partnership where two equals meet eye to eye, no dissolution of the self into the other, but rather a strengthening of who one is and who one can fully become because of the other. A partnership based in mutuality. Lodro and I consciously wrote this book in the belief that such partnership can and does exist.

We want to invite you into this dialogue. We are not self-professed experts on how to get that man or lady to fall in love with you. We are not therapists with an authoritative tone on how to have the perfect relationship. We are spiritual teachers. This book contains deeply personal, revealing, honest anecdotes to assist you with the inevitable ebb and flow of love in all its manifestations.

CHAPTER 1

HOW TO LOVE YOURSELF

Your task is not to seek for love, but merely to seek and find all the barriers within yourself that you have built against it.

—Helen Schucman, *A Course in Miracles*

When Everything Becomes Possible

MEGGAN

I was giving a talk while standing near the buffet table. Aromas of fried chicken and some sort of cheesy au gratin were distracting me. Well, that and the fact that every woman in the room that day was talking while she ate. Utensils were clanking, children were in various states of disarray from crying to running amid the tables, and my voice was only slightly more audible than the volume of their conversations. And I was just shy of shouting.

I had been invited to speak to a group of about 30 single mothers living with HIV. A single mom myself, I said yes in a heartbeat. They were being treated to a Mother's Day event of getting pampered and nourished in ways their daily lives didn't allow. I was talking about my experience working with pregnant teens, and how one teen in particular over a decade ago sent me on a spiritual journey by asking me to find "a more meaty Mary." Translation: an image of the divine that reflects the sacredness of the female body, the actual flesh. She wouldn't talk about God until I could give her an image of the divine that didn't make her feel worse about herself. She wanted an image she could identify with. I identified with her. I wanted to meet God's other half, too. I knew there had to be more. And I knew I wanted to consider my body as sacred. I just didn't have a clue as to how.

I told this lively group of ladies about the pilgrimage I made to sacred sites of the Black Madonna and Mary Magdalene throughout Europe. I recited as much of Marion Woodman's description of the Black Madonna as I could remember: "She is nature impregnated by spirit, accepting her own body as the chalice of the spirit. She has to do with the sacredness of matter; the intersection of sexuality and spirituality."[1] I thought maybe that would raise a few eyebrows, but there was no response. Not even a held glance.

I told them about the strange experiences I had at some of the sites, how I was brought to my knees from the weight of an unexpected love I found within me. And that this incited a revelation; encountering the divine means going within, means being fully in my body. But still, nada. Zilch. I told them about studying the Gospel of Mary Magdalene in seminary, how this was the "more meaty Mary" I wished the pregnant teen could have known. This Mary had very different ideas about the body and what it means to be female. Several women lifted their faces in my direction. But chaos continued to reign.

What made them set down their forks and wrestle their little ones into silence was my comment at the end— that ultimately the pilgrimage was not about finding an image of the divine feminine, a sacred site, or a truth somewhere that existed outside of me. The pilgrimage was ultimately about finding a source of love that had been with me all along. I told them that I traveled all that way, and studied theology for half a decade, only to find that the love I sought was actually within me. The room was thick with total, rapt attention.

Afterward, as I was signing copies of my first book, Reveal, for each lady, I noticed a woman who remained seated at a table in the far back, head bowed forward. I couldn't tell if she was filled with emotion, had fallen asleep during my talk, or was taking a mental moment to sort out her thoughts. I felt compelled to look up at her several times as I met the other women one by one. Once the room had cleared, she got up and walked toward me.

There was no introduction, no "Hello, my name is . . ." She walked right up to me and asked, "How can I find love inside me when I've never known love? I've known abuse. I've gotten beat up a lot. I'm a product of group homes. I've never had a home that's my own. But I'm still alive. So many of my friends have died. But I'm still here. When things start going good for me, I don't think I deserve it. And so it ends. But I want love. I do. I just can't find it."

I'm not sure which one of us teared up first. It was as if she'd grabbed my soul by the collar. I've never wanted to be able to body swap with someone more than in that moment. I wanted her to be me just for a second, to see herself through my eyes. Here she was saying that she couldn't find love and that she had never been shown love. And yet as she's saying this she's looking at me with eyes that are beaming out pure love with an intensity that was so bright it practically blinded me. I wanted her to see what I could see—that the presence of love was inside her. It seemed hard and painful for her to hold my gaze, but when her eyes finally did meet mine, I said, "I don't know what it will take for you to find love. But I see love inside you."

On my way home, I begged for all things holy to help this beautiful woman begin to feel the love that she contains. I didn't want her to have to wait another moment. I didn't want her to keep believing that someone else had to enter her life for the amount of love in her life to change. In Zen Buddhism, there's a practice in which the master gives the student a "koan," or a statement that tests the student's progress. The koan becomes a touchstone for the student's spiritual practice. And it elicits not so much a shift in thought but more a shift in being. On my pilgrimage, I would often hear this refrain while meditating: "Love, true love, means no longer waiting." It felt like this statement was a koan sent from my soul. And for a long time I had no bleeping clue what it meant. But that day on my way home, I remembered that koan and that feeling—when it seems like love is something outside of us, something we have to meet with, or earn, and so we wait. Talk about purgatory.

Many of us believe that love is something we have to "find." I've got a passport stamped up the wazoo to prove that I used to. What did it take to get me from believing love was something I had to search for outside of myself, to experiencing the love I already contain? What were those events or that singular thing that led me back to myself?

It began with a holy disdain for waiting. A sacred restlessness came over me every time I mapped out in my mind what more I had to do before I was *there*, meaning worthy of being loved. I became conscious of my daily addiction to the idea that I was almost-but-not-quite there. Just one more degree, one more relationship, one more notch on the proverbial belt and then . . . I'd be deserving. I would be that something more that I wasn't right now.

I've spent my life studying the world's religions. And the majority of them have been created around a solitary charismatic mystic. And each, no matter where in the globe or when in the span of human history, stumbled onto a golden rule . . . that we are to love each other as we love ourselves. On a certain level there's actually no difference between self-love and love of another. To love another is to love ourselves. And we are to do this not because of some external prompt. We are to love and be loved simply because this is what we are here to do.

"The Thunder, Perfect Mind" is an ancient manuscript that could date back as early as the 1st century B.C.E. It was found in the 20th century at Nag Hammadi along with about 50 other manuscripts that represent the Gnostic Gospels. It contains a divine feminine voice that seems to want to relate an all-encompassing presence that exists within each of us. Chapter 4, verses 30–31, reads, "Since what is your inside is your outside / And what you see on the outside, you see revealed on the inside."[2] This suggests that in our search for love the interior terrain is as crucial as what we witness and experience in the world around us. Our capacity to love another is directly proportional to our capacity to love ourselves.

For most, it starts outside of us. We begin to love ourselves because we are loved by another. Then—holy revelation—the time comes when that external source of love goes away or turns toxic. Perhaps after years of waiting for love, it still hasn't arrived and you've had it. Hopefully, you will realize that any and all outside sources of love are too inconsistent to rely on as your mainspring. You need *you*.

Ironically, I didn't meet with what's most eternal and sacred in me until I was at my most human. The two people I trusted I would grow old with, my son's father and my closest friend, needed to separate from me within the same year. I've never thought less of myself. For the two people who in many ways constituted my world to leave at once, well, let's just say it brought up every possible dark thought.

I had every external reason to believe that I wasn't "worthy" of love. And yet, this was when I finally chose to love me. I finally understood that I didn't actually need someone outside of me to truly understand the essence of who I am. That kind of validation had to come from within. I needed to trust in the unicorn of who I am. I needed to be the one who was there for myself, when no one else was.

How do we get there? The transformation happens by creating a miracle. I'm serious. It takes a miracle. But start small. And fake it until you make it. I started with gazing into my eyes in the bathroom mirror. At first, I laughed. Made jokes. ("Come here often?") But I stayed with it. And I began to focus not on those two blue irises but the presence of love that emerges from behind them.

It began. And then it grew. I met with that quiet yet steel-like presence of love within me whenever and wherever I could. I began to acknowledge that presence as my soul. And I started leaving it love notes. With a red Sharpie pen, I wrote on the mirror in the center of my wall altar, and on the long mirror where I check out my full-bodied look before going out:

i am divine love.

Each thought that was far from those love notes I left for my soul began to stand out as if clothed in neon colors in my mind. They couldn't just saunter in anymore like they owned the place. Now a fire alarm sounds whenever a negative thought about myself enters my mind, and I remember that thoughts are just thoughts. Some miracles come gradually. For me the miracle of recognizing my own love came little by little. But the utter transformation is nothing short of living revelation. Now I am love in action. For me this is the most radical thing I can do. The most powerful spiritual practice for me is the act of loving myself fiercely. Because in my experience, everything becomes possible when a person dares to meet with the love inside them. And so, I still sometimes whisper to myself, and to the spirit of that woman who wants so much to know love, that love, true love, means no longer waiting.

Your Love Is Indestructible

LODRO

For the last several years I have posed a simple question to people who want to talk about love and romance: "When you go out on a date, do you bring your most authentic you?" Ninety percent of the time, the response is "Hell, no." The idea of going out to a bar and truly being your own kind, wise self is desirable, but not one people often know how to pursue.

There is a reason for that. For one, people don't often see themselves as kind, wise, and desirable. Instead, many people think they are garbage. I hate even writing that word, but I have had meditation students approach me and say, "Who would want to be with me? I'm trash." I have had loved ones claim they were horrid or broken, even as I stood in front of them, loving them.

I have friends who, for the majority of their young adult lives, felt like they couldn't be themselves because of their sexual orientation. Raised Mormon, they were pushed into marrying a heterosexual mate, and ended up divorced because they were living a lie. I know others who embraced their homosexuality earlier than that and were kicked out of their conservative households. In both cases they were not able to be their most authentic selves until they came to terms with the fact that they were not confused; it was the people around them who had some inner work to do.

We either come up with reasons to doubt that we are inherently kind, wise, and desirable, or are told that by others. Either way we are grappling with something that is prevalent in society: self-doubt. Instead of embracing who we are, we give in to societal whispers telling us we're not good enough, lovable enough, or desirable enough. We are told we need products to scale higher rungs on the career ladder and then, when we attain that particular external factor, we will be happy. We are told we need to be different than who we actually are in this moment in order to free ourselves from this feeling of suffering. That is not the case.

When the Buddha sat down to meditate under the Bodhi Tree 2,600 years ago, he didn't sit down to come up with a master plan to make himself different. He acknowledged he was suffering and knew that he wanted to do something about that. He engaged in a simple meditation practice, which follows, to begin to look at that suffering. The more he looked, the more he realized that at his core, he wasn't basically messed up. He was basically good. He was basically awake. And he was not alone. We are, too. Our wakefulness is indestructible. It is like a diamond in a heap of dust. It is always there. We just need to discover it.

When we talk about the Buddha there is a Sanskrit term that is often used: he is the *Tathagata*. *Tathagata* can be translated as Buddha, but more directly as "the Awakened One." What did the Buddha wake up to? His own indestructible nature. He woke up his mind and heart in a very big way and woke up to reality as it is, as opposed to how he wished it were, or how it used to be. That is what we mean when we talk about meditation practice and attaining enlightenment. We are talking about how we can follow in the Buddha's footsteps by becoming more present and awake on the meditation seat and the rest of our day-to-day lives.

One of the things that the Buddha discovered was that he didn't have to bullshit. He saw reality for what it was, and was able to work with people and situations in a direct and genuine way. He wasn't a diplomat. He wasn't a politician. He was a revolutionary in that he presented himself authentically and people responded in kind. Whomever he met was inspired by his presence. Through the simple act of remaining openhearted, he invited people to join him in that space and be open-hearted as well. I mention this trait because we can do as the Buddha did and present ourselves authentically. In my experience there are three steps to this process:

1. Look at yourself

One of my favorite Tibetan words for "meditation" (there are several) is *gom*. *Gom* can also be translated as "familiarity." It is the notion that through the simple practice of being with the breath and watching your thoughts float across the landscape of your mind you are becoming more familiar with them. The more familiar you become with the various ways you get hooked by emotion, the habitual patterns that keep you running from the present moment, and the nonstop chatter going on in your head, the more familiar you become with the essence of who you are.

2. Discover your basic goodness

When you become familiar with the essence of who you are, you see what the Buddha saw: you are not basically messed up. You see that beyond whatever layers of confusion and pain that have developed over the years you are innately peaceful. You are inherently wise, good, and strong. That is your true nature, what is referred to within my tradition of Shambhala as "basic goodness." Basic goodness is the experience that you are primordially whole. That is who you are. And it's not just you; everyone else possesses this same nature. As Meggan said, this idea of love is not something we have to "find." It's already within us. We have to experience it, in that know-it-in-your-gut sort of way.

3. Develop faith in that goodness

Once you have glimpsed that you are basically good, you should develop faith in that. It's easy to give in to internal or external whispers that you're basically not good enough, but if you can experience this sense of primordial wholesomeness, then that can trump whatever gets thrown at you. It's not an idea, like the idea that you need a new iPad, but an understanding. We can have faith in our experience of basic goodness and continue to cultivate that both on and off the meditation cushion.

As you engage this process you are learning to have faith in yourself and offer yourself fully, as you are. Even if you have never meditated a day in your life, I am guessing you have already had this particular experience and know the benefits of it. There you are, fighting with your partner and throwing accusations at each other. "You did this and it hurt me," and "I don't know what you want from me," and "Why do I always have to do these things you never do?" Those old go-to's. Then you drop the defensive act, relax your body, look your lover in the eyes, and say, "I'm so sorry I hurt you. I love you and never want to do that." By letting down your guard you are inviting your partner to do the same. You are relinquishing the habitual desire to struggle. More often than not, this is the tipping point in an argument where love wins out over aggression.

Imagine what that tactic of authenticity would do in other situations. Your boss is being a jerk, and you pause and respond with an open heart. Or your mother is hinting that you don't want to spend time with her, and you tell her how much you appreciate her. Or you go to a bar and instead of trying to convince people they should like you, you are genuine and people become attracted to that.

I am reminded of a time some years ago when I was out with some friends and met a lovely woman. We flirted a bit, she joined our group for some drinks, and then she gave me her number and kissed me before heading home. My friend turned to me; clearly something was on her mind. "What did you say to land a girl like that?" she asked. No one had ever called me on my flirting ability. I had no real answer. The first thing that came to mind, which I'll stand by, was "I was just genuinely me. I think people like genuine."

The essence of who you are is innately lovable. When we drop the constant critiques that come up throughout our day, we experience a sense of peace and warmth. We learn to love ourselves. Most of the time we walk around thinking, *I wish I hadn't said that,* or *I really need to do that better next time.* Rarely do we sit down and appreciate all the good we have done. All too rarely do we celebrate our human potential.

The beauty of the meditation practice I introduce at the end of this chapter is that it is a simple tool for doing just that. Yes, we become familiar with both the sanity and insanity that rages in our mind through meditation, but we also get glimpses that we are lovely human beings. We see that we don't need to rely on a new product or job or even romantic partner to be whole. My Buddhist teacher, Sakyong Mipham Rinpoche, wrote, "True love is the natural energy of our settled mind."[3] Through training in being with something as simple as the breath, you are learning to settle down with yourself and also training in being with your inherent wakefulness. Within our natural state there is unfathomable love. That is what the Buddha discovered and what you can discover as well.

The Tibetan Buddhist teacher Pema Chödrön once wrote, "I can't overestimate the importance of accepting ourselves exactly as we are right now, not as we wish we were or think we ought to be."[4] If we want to be in relationship to others, step one is self-acceptance and self-love. The most important thing we can do is go down the same road as the Buddha and engage a process of self-discovery. When we do that we learn to accept ourselves as we are right now, not as some puffed-up version of ourselves that might be more lovable or attractive to others. We discover who we are, and then radiate that truth out to the world.

Meditation

From Meggan

All meditation is ultimately an attempt to clear away the obstacles that block the flow of our own love. I do this by focusing all of my attention into my heart. The heart for me is a sanctuary, an inner temple where I can meet with what is eternal. I refer to this contemplative practice as the soul-voice meditation. What is crucial to notice during this practice is if there are any places within you that still carry the thought or judgment that you are unworthy.

Imagine that even the darkest moments in your life have profound teachings to give you, instead of more "baggage" than you or even a partner could carry. See both the happy and the hard moments of your life as opportunities for you to acquire more of the precise attributes to flex and exercise your capacity to love.

Sit still and clearly feel your awareness anchor down into your heart. Then, ask your soul, "Where has my love not yet reached?" Resist nothing. Invite all of those hard-to-reach stories to come back to you. Trust that you are ready to see and receive them in a new way. Maybe you see a bully from high school who humiliated you. Maybe you remember when you were not there for someone in their time of need, and so you still hold regret and guilt. Maybe you have believed all this time someone else's truth about you—for example, that you are in some way not good enough, or too much for anyone to handle. One by one allow these memories, these stories, to return to you. And invite them in like dinner guests.

Now, here's how we shift these stories and beliefs about ourselves from what holds us back to deeper amounts of love. Forgive yourself. Love yourself by letting these stories go. I know what I'm asking you to do because I know just how hard it is. I do it daily. Initially, it felt like moving through stone. But over the years, it has become far more light filled. I go within, I ask to see where my love has not yet reached. And when that moment or aspect of myself reveals itself—like for example, feeling unworthy of a spiritual life partner because of how long it has taken me to know my own worth—I embrace it with open arms, and with a comment like "Well, look at you!" And I love it; I love myself regardless, which is all that feeling of unworthiness needs to—*poof!*—disappear.

If you are having a hard time bringing love to a particular memory or moment because that limiting belief is just too convincing, then go back to a moment when you felt utterly and completely loved, even if that moment was fleeting. Practice as often as possible allowing the moment to suffuse you with the warmth and honeylike sweetness of knowing that you are beloved just as you are.

Then go back to that hard-to-forgive moment or that limiting belief about yourself and let love organically morph your guilt or regret into pure forgiveness. How will you know if you have really released? Waves of love will wash over you and you will most likely do the ugly cry. You will feel a sense of being brought to your knees from the weight of your own love returning to you.

If you love to write like I do, then try writing out all the stories, all the excuses you have held tight to about why you don't deserve love. Let them live in your journal rather than within you. Pay attention to the stories that still feel alive to you even now.

For each of those moments, ask yourself if there is anything left you can learn from them. And ask if there is anything left for you to forgive. What stories are held as if in Tupperware containers in your heart? Where can love yet reach within you?

FROM LODRO

The type of meditation I recommend to launch your journey of self-discovery is called *shamatha*, or calm-abiding meditation. It is a bit of a misnomer in that when you first sit down to meditate it may not feel calm. It may feel a bit chaotic and hard to stay with the object of your meditation. This is natural. It's like learning a new instrument or sport; at first you're figuring out how to do it, but after a bit of practice it almost feels second nature to you.

The first step is to find a comfortable place within which to meditate. At the time of this writing I am traveling in Colorado and Utah, and my friends seem to have rooms that are not their bedroom, living room, or bathroom, but could actually accommodate a space for meditation. As a New Yorker, this is strange to me. My personal meditation space is a corner of my living room. Whether you can devote a room or a corner of a room, we all have some spot where we can sit down and not get distracted. So wheel your TV out of view, put your phone aside, close your laptop, and sit down on a cushion or chair about four to six feet away from the wall.

If you are on a cushion, be it your pillow, something you pulled from your couch, or a formal meditation seat, sit in the center of it with your legs loosely crossed and your knees a bit lower than your hips. If you are sitting on a chair, place yourself in the center of that, sitting up and away from the back of it and placing your feet firmly on the ground about hip-width apart. You want to feel grounded when you sit down to meditate.

Take a moment to relax into your body. It took me more years than I'd care to admit to realize that meditation is a physical practice, not a mental one. Check in with your physical form, doing a quick body scan or by taking a few deep breaths. After running around all day, your body and mind may feel like you've been going 100 miles per hour. See if you can get yourself down to, at most, 80 at this point.

From this strong base you can elongate your spine, extending your body upward. Leading from your head, pull your upper body toward the sky, such that your spine becomes like a stack of quarters, one vertebra on top of the other, all the way up. We don't need to force the muscles in our back or shoulders to achieve this upright status. We relax with our natural skeletal curvature.

Drop your hands at your side. Then, picking them up from the elbows, drop them palms down on your thighs. This should be a comfortable place to rest them and will give you extra support for your back, given that we are not often accustomed to sitting up straight. Your head rests at the top of your spine, and you can tuck in your chin very slightly.

Relax the muscles in your face, including those around your forehead, around your eyes, and in your jaw. This may mean that your jaw hangs open, which is great. You can even place your tongue up against the roof of your mouth to allow for clear breathing. Finally, rest your gaze about two to four feet in front of you. Keep your gaze loose and unfocused. The view here is that we are doing what the Buddha did: we are waking up our mind and heart in a big way. Why should we close our eyes if we are trying to wake up? It seems counter to our intention. So try keeping your eyes open for this meditation session.

In shamatha meditation the object of our focus is the breath. We are learning to be present with something that we do all the time, so that we can be more present with more complex things down the road, like romance. What I am asking you to do is to pay full attention to the physical sensation of both the out breath and the in breath. Tune in to the natural cycle of your breathing. You don't need to alter the breath at all; we are learning to be with who we are and what is, so let your breath go as it always does. Ride the fluid and peaceful nature of the breath.

After a few moments you will get distracted. I almost said "may," but unfortunately we are not accustomed to being present with something as simple as the breath, and our mind gets antsy and wants to do other things. It drifts off into the future, making plans for the weekend, or relives that text exchange you had with your crush. When you notice that a large thought has taken you out of the room, exercise gentleness by silently saying "thinking" to yourself. Use this word as a reminder that what you really want to do is be with the breath. You have caught yourself drifting off into thoughts, so say "thinking," and then use that word as an opportunity to come back to the present moment.

Try the shamatha meditation as described above for ten minutes. Set a timer to go off after that time so you don't have to constantly glance at your watch. At the end of that meditation period you may feel refreshed or exhausted. You may have caught a glimpse of peace, that basic goodness I mentioned above, or you may have spent ten minutes frustrated that you could barely stay with the breath.

Sakyong Mipham Rinpoche has said in many of his talks, "Any meditation is good meditation." When you are done with your meditation session, don't judge it as good or bad. It is all a process of becoming more familiar with yourself. It can feel a bit like when you have started dating someone; sometimes it's awesome and then sometimes you hit uncomfortable moments or get into a fight. In either case you can appreciate it because you are learning more about the other person. Here you can say the same thing in regards to learning more about yourself. Any time you spend with yourself is a good time, regardless of whether you find it pleasurable or painful. With that in mind, try sitting in this meditation form for ten minutes a day going forward as you read this book, utilizing it as one of many ways we will learn to love ourselves more fully.

When you begin to familiarize yourself with yourself, and discover glimpses of basic goodness, you see you are okay just as you are. At your core you are good. You are strong. You are wise. You are worthy of love and to love. That is your birthright. Once you discover that, it becomes hazy as to why you would try and hide who you are.

There is one last Tibetan word I want to share in this regard: *ziji*. In its most common translation it can be "confidence." You can grow confident in who you are and share yourself authentically with others. That is something you can always do, as you become familiar with yourself. Another way *ziji* is translated is "radiating splendor." When you are confident in who you are, in your own ability to befriend and love yourself, that radiates out into the world. The most attractive thing is when someone is confident in who they are and is willing to share it with the world. Radiate your splendor as part of loving yourself.

CHAPTER 2

How to Love Being Single

There is no need to struggle to be free; the absence of struggle is in itself freedom.

—Chögyam Trungpa Rinpoche

Single, Free, and Wild

LODRO

A long while ago I went on a first date. We met online—a new thing for me, something I supposedly was doing in the name of research. I arrived at the bar on time, but she had texted me 12 minutes prior, letting me know she was already there. I greeted her warmly, and asked how she was. "Fine," she said, "although I didn't like sitting alone at a bar for twelve minutes."

We went on to have a perfectly nice time together, but the next day this one comment was still with me. Why was she unable to be alone for 12 minutes? It's not that a lot of men were hitting on her, which might have explained her discomfort period (The bar was mostly empty.) If I had to venture a guess, I would say it was because she was left to look at her own mind in a potentially anxiety-producing situation: a first date. She was looking for a distraction.

I don't mean to pick on my date. I would be remiss if I didn't mention that she had a tattoo that looked dangerously like Hitler, but she was very nice and exemplified something we all do. We have habituated ourselves to run from discomfort, and being alone doesn't necessarily feel good. We desire distraction at these times. Since the advent of cell phones, many of us have discovered that we don't have to be alone—ever. If you sit down at a bar, or ride a subway, or are in an elevator, you can just take out your phone and connect with another person you know (or meet someone new).

In fact, it's not uncommon to see people out in a social setting clicking away on their phones, reaching out to new people online instead of trying to meet other people where they are. When we reach out in this way we are no longer alone with our own minds and hearts. It seems to me that the amount of time we reserve for actually being by ourselves in the present moment has become less and less, as a result of the various tools we have for connecting instantly with others. Being alone has become foreign to us.

There's a reason our distraction technology is so popular: When we are left to our own devices it can, at times, be uncomfortable. We don't like discomfort. The Buddhist author and nun Pema Chödrön has said, "As a species, we should never underestimate our low tolerance for discomfort. To be encouraged to stay with our vulnerability is news that we can use."[1]

I had barely met this woman, so I wasn't about to quote Pema at her (and what an obnoxious thing to do on a first date). But I think we all need some encouragement to stay with our experience of being alone. We need to explore what it feels like to be vulnerable, to be by ourselves. We should realize it's okay to be uncomfortable.

Things that are uncomfortable for some people are wonderfully luxurious for others, if they can relax into them. Seven years ago I enjoyed my first solitary drink. I remember it well. Living in Boston, I frequented Matt Murphy's Pub. That particular evening, my friends were all busy and my favorite bartender had the night off. I sat down at the bar alone. The place was so empty I wondered what I was doing there. I had that moment of distinct discomfort. But after a few words the bartender slowly poured my Auchentoshan scotch. I paused. Something felt familiar.

At that point I had already spent a lot of time in solitary meditation retreats. I had glimpsed the joy that comes from spending time alone. That evening, after spending the whole day running from one meeting to the next, squeezing in e-mails and phone calls, and speaking with lots of people, I had a chance to be alone again. I took a moment to contemplate what that meant for me, and it became clear: this drink was my moment of solitude.

Even if I can't always run off to the woods and lock myself up for weeks on end in silent retreat, I can still enjoy time on the meditation cushion or a solitary drink. Drinking can mean different things to different people: some people drink to escape, some to celebrate, some to cover over their pain. For me, in that moment, the drink was a means to carve out some time to be alone. It was a time for self-reflection. There's something magical about that experience that I have returned to many times since. My favorite author, Raymond Chandler, wrote of it: "I like the neat bottles on the bar back and the lovely shining glasses and the anticipation. I like to watch the man mix the first one of the evening and put it down on a crisp mat and put the little folded napkin beside it. I like to taste it slowly. The first quiet drink of the evening in a quiet bar—that's wonderful."[2]

This description by Chandler celebrates being alone. I used the example of being at a bar but it could just as well be a quiet meal at a restaurant or spending an afternoon at a flea market. There is the liberation of getting home from work and knowing you can do anything you want, without having to check in with anyone. There is the joy of sitting in a bookstore or a movie theater on a Sunday afternoon and knowing it's okay to not chat with others. There is contentment in curling up with a good book on the beach, feeling the sand between your toes and knowing that there isn't a soul who even knows where you are. When we embrace being alone, it is freeing.

The Buddhist teacher Chögyam Trungpa Rinpoche talked about this form of romantic freedom in his book *Work, Sex, Money.* He drew a distinction between "free-free" and "free-wild." "Free-free" is the form of freedom I mentioned above; you are not freed by anyone else, but by the discovery that you are free to do whatever you might desire. You embrace the space of your life and play within it. The contrasting form of freedom he mentions is "free-wild." "Free-wild" is when you define your freedom in relationship to others. You can't deal with space in your life so you fill up your free time with all sorts of distractions. There is a frantic nature to how you spend your time. He said, "It is wild in the sense of neurotic . . . You are creating your own imprisonment under the pretense of freedom."[3]

How often do you imprison yourself under this pretense of being free? I have certainly done it before. I am what is commonly referred to as a serial monogamist. I have bounced between long-term relationships for the last 12-plus years with only minimal healing time in between. After some of these breakups I would commit to taking time off from dating, but then immediately get distracted from that goal of spending time alone and fall into another romance before I was ready. Finally, the big emotional upset of a broken engagement gave me pause and (admittedly after a few stumbling blocks) I realized that what I needed to do was take the time to be alone. I needed to be free-free.

Here's the thing about officially committing to being single: as soon as you do, every desirable person you would ever be attracted to automatically gravitates toward you. I don't know if you have experienced this phenomenon, but it's as if you tell the universe, *I need to be alone*, and it sends you the hottest, sexiest, most brilliant creature to convince you otherwise. As a result, I discovered that I needed to actually apply discipline to the simple act of taking time to become more familiar with myself.

Discipline is not unfamiliar. As a longtime meditator I have the discipline of getting to the meditation cushion every day and of exerting myself in my practice. There are times when I have applied the same discipline to other areas of my life: exercising more regularly, or eating better, or writing consistently. I have trained myself to be quite good at discipline, and to treat it as a positive force in my life.

However, when it comes to the discipline of renunciation I'm still learning. In the stories I've shared so far you can see that I have been good about the discipline of adding things to my life, but now I was in a period of time where I had to cut something out: romantic distraction. There were several good reasons for this decision. I needed the time to nurse a broken heart, to reexamine my dating habits, to concentrate on befriending myself more deeply. Yet I found it hard not to get distracted. I found it hard to not go free-wild.

Free-wild can come in many forms. For some people (read: me) it might mean going out every night. For others it might be going on online dating sites. For still others it could be holing up at home and binge watching television and griping that there are no good people to date. There are so many ways we distract ourselves from ourselves.

What if you didn't do that? What if you applied discipline to really befriending yourself? I realize that what I am suggesting is vaguely countercultural. We are not generally encouraged to just be with what's going on and look at our own mind. But that is the beauty of meditation practice. You become more familiar with who you are and all of the ways that you try to distract yourself.

When you are single, you can take the free-free mind-set or the free-wild mind-set. You can say, *This is nice. I have a chance to get to know myself and am going to exert myself in doing that.* That is the discipline practice I am suggesting. Or you can say, *I need to find someone to love.* There are a million parties and bars and dating sites to feed into the free-wild mind-set. You can even go on Tinder or Grindr—apps on your phone—and while you are waiting for your date or the subway, or on the elevator, take those short periods of time to match and flirt with strangers. We have made it very easy to get free-wild. But after a hundred or more Tinder/Grindr matches (or as one friend calls them, "Tinder boos"), you have to ask yourself: do you feel any more comfortable in your own skin?

I doubt it. With these distractions, it's not unlike waking up next to someone in your bed and regretting the experience. You were alone, it got to a point where it was too uncomfortable, you reached out to someone, slept with him or her, and yet the next day you feel even more alone. You can have this experience with Tinder boos, or a week full of parties. You keep waking up, physically alone or not, but with the realization that the distraction you are employing just isn't working. Dating becomes a form of entertainment, a distraction from the loneliness or other emotions that are playing across our mind like the clouds play across the sky.

I often joke with new meditation students that in all likelihood they are trying meditation because they have already tried everything else. So many of us look to alcohol or drugs or romance or online shopping to make us feel good about ourselves. And so many of us realize those aren't lasting solutions. At the end of the day, we need to get comfortable being with ourselves and embracing ourselves, as we are. One of the reasons I meditate is because it's a great way to get to know my own mind, including all the ways I feed this free-wild mind-set.

The meditation practice, as previously described, is quite simple. You sit there, resting with the natural flow of the breath. The most active part of the process is your own mind. Your mind wanders around all the things you could be doing, making lists for what you will do when you get done or reliving conversations with someone you're attracted to. *What did he mean by that? When can I see her again?* Yet over and over you apply the discipline to come back to what is actually going on, which is your breathing.

The interesting thing is that meditation practice is practice for the rest of your life. You are training in being with reality as it is. As Chögyam Trungpa Rinpoche has said, "You have to become familiar with the desires;

then the need to express them physically automatically wears out."[4] It's like an alcoholic beginning the process of recovery. The first step is to realize that you have a problem. Then you can do something about it. Once you have admitted your addiction, you can recover from it.

In our case, we are addicted to distraction. Through the process of meditation we become familiar with our myriad desires, and all of the ways we habitually distract ourselves. The more familiar we become, the more the need to physically act out dissipates. We start to see that if we feel lonely we can be with the reality of our loneliness; we don't have to do something about it. Loneliness is so incredibly human. We don't have to line up a date with someone we're feeling so-so about, or rush out the door to connect with others. We can simply be with our loneliness. We can remain free-free by applying the discipline of resting with what is.

Some of us may feel like we've done our time being alone. We have gotten pretty familiar with ourselves, and now we're ready to meet someone. That is a good thing to discern, and it gives us another opportunity to become more familiar with our own mind and to discover our personal pendulums of hope and fear.

In some sense, I could just say "personal pendulums of fear and fear" here, as set versions of hope and fear are really two sides of the same coin. When you are going to the beach you hope for good weather, right? One could invert that and say that you fear rain. If you hope to meet the love of your life, you might also on some level fear you will never meet such a person. We fluctuate often between hope and fear, depending on our mood, thinking something might work out or it never will. It sounds pretty miserable, right? Later on, Meggan will get into a more disciplined form of hope that can prove invaluable to us.

I remember going through a particularly brutal breakup and thinking, *I'm not sure I'll meet anyone like her ever again.* It's true; I doubt I will, as she is a unique individual. But the despair with which I thought this . . . oh man! It was all-pervasive. I was wallowing in my own self-doubt and feelings of worthlessness. I thought I had blown my one shot at happiness. In my heart of hearts, I knew that happiness is not dependent on other people, but in that moment it was overshadowed by my fear.

This was a time when meditation was particularly useful. I came back to the basic training of being with what is actually going on. My practice on the cushion was sitting with a broken heart as well as feelings of inadequacy, fear of loving again, and some glimmer of hope that maybe we would work things out. That hope, of course, was also a fear that we wouldn't. While I was single and free to date anyone I pleased, the time spent off the meditation cushion was free-wild—I was trying to avoid my feelings by filling up space.

Over time it became easier to rest with who I am, including all of the yucky and uncertain parts of my life. Even if I couldn't convince myself that I would find someone I would want to date, I could rest with the idea that I didn't need to "fix" anything. I could be alone and learn to love myself.

At each stage in our romantic journey we need to discover one simple truth: it's okay to love ourselves. It's the building block we need in place before we can go on to love others. That means that before we connect with our date, we should be okay sitting at the bar for 12 minutes. It also means that when we're heartbroken or ready to love again, it's okay to spend time with ourselves. We don't need to churn up activity and distractions in order to make things happen. Things happen in their own time. Our job is to prepare ourselves, to learn to love ourselves, in this time in between. Whether you are commuting, at a bar, or in an elevator, you can put your phone down and look up. Rest your mind. Befriend yourself.

Indie Mom

MEGGAN

I still can't figure out exactly how it happened. But I guess when it's time to meet a teacher, that teacher can appear in the most unexpected way.

By the summer of 2012, I had been separated from my husband for two years. And the divorce was official. I had gone on some dates (more about that later) but didn't yet feel a real sense or at least a positive sense of being "free." I cringed at the moniker *single mom*. And I couldn't embrace the reality that I was on my own again.

Unlike the Hitler-tattoo lady that Lodro mentioned, I am very good at being alone. Almost too good. I have the constitution of a cloistered nun. I could be walled up in some abbey high in the mountains and be happy as a clam. I know how to work on myself and to be free-free. I felt excitement when I met my husband because it finally felt like I was trying something new: being free together.

I wasn't anxious about being alone after the divorce; I had that bit on autopilot. It was just that every once in a while, a trapdoor would open up beneath my heart, and I suddenly felt like the walking dead. The sense that I could make meaning of the loss of my marriage and this heartbreak left me, and despair took its place. I would hear myself lament, "I am never going to stop loving him." It hit me as the truth, and I felt trapped—stuck in the wake of an unrequited love.

Enter Captain Tom. At that time, I was beginning to travel for speaking events. I had already flown to California that spring, and now I wanted to fly to Vancouver. I had taken an online video course called SOAR, which had helped tremendously with my flight out west. The founder of SOAR, Captain Tom Bunn, is an experienced commercial pilot who had such compassion for those of us with fear of flying (picture me, a hot panicked mess, running off airplanes at the last minute) that he got his master's degree in social work and came up with a way to powerfully reduce stress for phobic fliers. I reached out to him to get some more support before my first solo flight out of the country in over a decade.

I entered the name Tom in my Gmail search engine and up popped an e-mail address. I sent off an e-mail asking if we could arrange a call. It began, *Dear Captain Tom . . .* I got a quick response from an assistant. He replied that Tom was busy but wanted to help in any way he could. He asked for my cell number and said Tom would call in the next couple days. *Huh,* I thought. *How odd not to have a more fixed system in place for one-on-one business calls.* But I shrugged it off and responded with gratitude.

A couple of days later, as I was wrestling my son out of his jammies and into some clothes (something he still resists with his whole being), my cell phone rang. It was an unrecognized number out of California.

"Hey. This is Tom."

"Tom? Captain Tom? Oh, thank you for calling."

"Sure. How can I help?"

At this point there was an epically long silence. First of all, I had a sinking feeling that this wasn't the Tom I had set out to speak with but I wasn't sure why. Second, I was still trying to get my son's pants on while debating in my mind about whether or not to ask Captain Tom why he was calling from California when he lived in Connecticut. But then, I did the absolute best thing—I just went with it.

Thus began one of the most powerful conversations I have ever had about the nature of fear and the inner resources we have to choose love instead. There were times in the hour-long call when I was convinced that this was the Captain Tom I knew . . . I mean, who else could it be? But then Tom started in on a dialogue that left me certain I was not speaking to the retired airline pilot turned social worker from SOAR.

After telling him about my various and hilarious encounters with extreme fear on airplanes, Unknown Tom asked, "So what do you think this fear of flying is really about?" I told him the conclusions I had come to about the fear—that the physical reality of flight, being trapped on that aluminum tube at crazy speeds and heights, triggered my awareness of just how vulnerable and out of control I am at all times. And that this awareness created a fear so large I lost all sight and sense of being a soul. I disassociated. So the external heights of being on a flight were actually less distressing than the internal distance fear created between my body and soul.

Unknown Tom made a thoughtful noise that let me know he understood, that he was right there with me. Then he asked, "Is there some part of you that believes you have to be perfect or 'fixed' before you can be loved?" My jaw dropped. Unknown Tom continued, "The beauty of the masculine is that it can hold the feminine no matter what the circumstances. There's nothing that needs to be done or perfected."

Here was the truth! I sat down on my red couch. It felt like I had to recover from a spiritual punch to the gut. There was some part of me that was desperately trying to be "more" or "better" than I had been when I was married. Self-improvement and personal growth are great. But what Unknown Tom revealed to me is that fear was motivating me; fear was allowing me to unconsciously believe that I was unlovable until I became a "better" woman. I could see then that there was a part of me that blamed myself for not being enough. As if my marriage would have lasted if I had been more. Better. Less afraid. When in truth, I didn't believe that love was earned or that we had to demonstrate we are worthy of love. Love is beyond our conscious reasoning.

I didn't have a man in my life, not yet, but the compassionate, nonjudgmental way Unknown Tom held me throughout the conversation reminded me that I am entirely lovable right now, as I am. And that I can flex the inner masculine within me and hold myself through this transitional time in my life in a way I never have before. I can cultivate a love with a hairy chest and big bulging biceps, a love that holds me where I am broken or when I am scared. It's not enough to know that I am enough; I have to put that knowing into action. At the end of our call, Unknown Tom said that I had three spiritual assignments, "Trust, trust, and trust." "Yes," I agreed.

When I hung up the phone, I was amazed at how entirely met I felt, how much forgiveness I had for where I was, and how grateful. I raced to my computer and typed Tom into my Gmail search engine to recover the thread of e-mails that had led to the call. I clicked on the down arrow to see the full e-mail address of the Tom I had contacted—and there it was. His last name. Shady-ac. I'd just had one of the most intimate, spiritual conversations with Tom Shadyac, the film director of *Bruce Almighty* and many other blockbuster hits as well as a film I had seen recently titled *I Am*. He had also published a book with Hay House, and Gmail had saved his e-mail address from a group e-mail sent to authors. I got out my red Sharpie and wrote on the gilded mirror near where I write each day: *Trust, trust, and trust.* And I attributed the quote to Captain Tom.

In The Gospel of Mary Magdalene, translated by Harvard scholar Dr. Karen King, Mary comforts the other disciples who fear for their lives now that Jesus, or the Savior, had been crucified. She stands up, greets them, tenderly kisses them all, and then says, "Brothers and sisters, do not be distressed nor be in doubt. For his grace will be with you sheltering you. Rather we should praise his greatness, for he has united us and made us true Human beings."[5]

This passage has always reminded me of an ultimate spiritual goal of mine: to be a true human being. In Mary Magdalene's Gospel, a true human being is someone (male or female) who has realized his or her inner divinity. Someone who is, yes, fully human—capable of base emotions and huge mistakes, but also fully divine. A true human being is conscious of the creative power within to align ourselves with the life lessons our soul needs most, a power that begins with any thought that starts, *I am . . .*

So as I waded through the very human flotsam in the wake of divorce, and I stayed anchored in the trust of the divine love within me. I didn't forget that even in the midst of this love lost, there is a love within that I can always connect to and receive—a divine love that is the most stabilizing force to depend on, no matter what is happening in my external world.

Several weeks later, I was riding in a gondola up Mt. Whistler Mountain with another speaker from the event. She is also an author and a divorced mom raising a son. I refer to her as the High Priestess of Desire. The vista at the top of the mountain was breathtaking. Snow glistened at the peak. I felt a sudden surge of adventure, climbed up the steep incline, and then slid down (sans sled), picking up more momentum than anticipated. I laughed harder than I had in years. The High Priestess of Desire took a picture of me just as I reached the rocks where she was standing. I was amazed when I saw it. It barely looked like me. Or rather it looked like me from seven years ago before my marriage to a man who tried but couldn't commit to partnership. I looked free. My face was radiating light. I was in love. Not with someone, but just in love as I am. For me this picture marked the moment when I removed the moniker *single mom* from my thoughts and all the sadness and despair that went with it. This is the moment I became an *indie mom*.

As an indie mom, I could feel the adventure inherent in being free, and independent. I felt excitement rather than fear about what's next, and who's next. As an indie mom, I reinterpreted the old lament *I am never going to stop loving him* into an affirmation that reflects the woman I am and will always be: I am someone who loves with her entire being. I can continue to love my son's father no matter what. My love for him is mine. I can love him as an invaluable friend, and as a father to our miraculous son. I can love him as the soul who has given me so many opportunities to strengthen my own capacity to love. I am never going to stop loving him because that is true to who I am.

Proverbs 13:12 reads, "Hope deferred makes the heart sick, but a longing fulfilled is the tree of life." There's no way around the pure desire I have for a life partner, for my soul to meet her match. I long for it with ardor. Over the past four years that I've been an indie mom, it has always been clear to me that I desire a relationship. I feel fulfilled in partnership in ways that I don't on my own. I know I want a life partner. And I honor that knowing. Yet, at the same time, I know that divine love is always here, entirely present within me. So I began to wonder: *How do I feel whole while still leaving space in my life for the love of my life to enter? How do I feel fulfilled and yet be authentic to the desire I have to share my life with a partner? How do I wait without waiting?* And the answer I came up with is a spiritual practice that I call Disciplined Hope.

Hope as a noun is synonymous with a wish, or an aspiration. But hope as a verb is synonymous with an expectation, or even a prediction. Disciplined Hope isn't just wishing things were different or wishing for something to enter our lives. When I really focused on how much I wished there was someone with me in those tender, unrepeatable moments, like when my son first walked, or when I signed my first book contract, I would despair. I would feel an acute sense of loss and lack in my life. I would feel very much alone. But Disciplined Hope isn't just wishing, it's putting that hope into action, it's trusting that at some point that pure desire to love and be loved will be met. So what does hope in action look like? How do I wait without waiting as an indie mom?

I tango. One of the ways I practice Disciplined Hope is that I experience surrender in couples dancing. I took to tango like any Scorpio would—passionately. What my tango teacher explained to me was that surrender is active. He explained that if I'm limp and passive, I'm not giving him the presence he needs to be able to move me. If I "arrive" at each step he guides me to, if I stay present in the moment, stay fully in my body, he is able to direct our dance with ease. This physical experience of being held and led in tango allows me to taste an essence of partnership now.

Disciplined Hope is trusting my life fiercely, all that has happened. It's trusting who I am, that I am enough right now. And it's trusting where I am being led. It's putting trust in my life into practice that at some divinely timed moment, my desire is going to be met.

Suggestions for embracing being free-free and practicing Disciplined Hope

From Lodro

1. I go to the sauna to release toxins, take care of my body, and be alone with my thoughts.

2. I take nights in to smoke a tobacco pipe and drink one whiskey, to rest with whatever has been coming up for me that week.

3. I read silly novels. Sometimes comic books. Okay, a lot of comic books. It reminds me of simpler times in my life and lets me reflect on my past.

4. I go for long drives or train rides, listening to bad pop music and enjoying the scenery and the feeling that no one knows where I am but me.

5. I take a long walk with my puppy, who is very adorable and offers unconditional love without much communication.

FROM MEGGAN

1. I get regular massages (always by male masseurs) so that my body isn't starved for touch.

2. I plan dinners with friends and weekends away when my son is with his father.

3. I pay conscious attention to how much love I have in my life (in all its various forms).

4. I pour myself into my work, which is my soul purpose.

5. I use those moments when the trapdoor swings open and my heart starts to plummet to actively connect to the divine source of love and truth within me.

CHAPTER 3

HowtoLoveDating

> Believe in a love that is being stored up for you like
> an inheritance, and have faith that in this love there is
> a strength and a blessing so large that you can travel as
> far as you wish without having to step outside it.

—Rainer Maria Rilke, *Letters to a Young Poet*

The Dream and the Not-Quite-Rights

Meggan

I was sitting at the bar debating about whether or not to order a glass of red wine. I'm a lightweight (all it takes is one glass on an empty stomach) and the last thing I wanted was to be lit when my blind date walked through the door. I had been married and divorced and yet I had never officially "dated" before.

My life up until that point had been a succession of monogamous relationships that just sort of happened once I was ready for them. I never went out looking for them. Each next partner just arrived. At work, at divinity school, at seminary, at a grocery store (the organic section, no less). I trusted myself and my life enough to lead me to the love I needed. Divorce humbled me. It indelibly severed my ego's idea that I know what's best for me. It reminded me that my soul holds a deeper knowing than my conscious reasoning. And it allowed me to question everything. To reinvent myself. To try new things. To cast a far wider net. So when my mom gifted me a membership to a blind-dating service for New

Yorkers, I held back my initial gut response (a wildly loud *NO!*) and decided to say yes to what I hadn't tried before. That's how in my midthirties I found myself sitting on a barstool about to have a blind date for the first time. And I was feeling really proud of myself. And excited. That is, right up until a man who looked *exactly* like my dad walked into the bar, caught my eye, and came swiftly over to introduce himself; yep, my date.

To be fair to my dad's doppelgänger, I had a really great night. Yes, he was 20-plus years my senior, but he was brilliant, funny, extremely successful, and ready to meet a woman he could share his life with. It really wasn't so much his age that made a second date impossible. I had once been in a powerful relationship with a man 19 years older than me. It was more that my dad's look-alike was in another stage in life. I didn't know yet if I wanted to have another child, but I knew I wanted the possibility to be there. So when I got home, paid the babysitter, and kissed my son's impossibly sweet-smelling forehead, I tempered my pride in trying something new with wondering if my openness should have its limits.

My cousin Michael and I would often meet for what we called Family Dinner (or Fam Din, while texting). We were both in NYC and we were the only two in our immediate family who weren't married or in a committed relationship. We were also the types who would prefer to be hermits rather than really put ourselves out there. I remember one particular Fam Din when Michael referred to the man he was dating as "my David." He was helping me get over the slight trauma of my blind-date dad when I got confused about who he was referring to because my dad's name is David and so is his boyfriend's. Then he laughed and said, "my David." The soft tone to his voice let me know he was in it for the long haul.

I asked him to tell me about his David and explain why he wasn't just another boyfriend. Over avocado rolls and vegetable maki, I listened intently as Michael described how he knew that this love was it: there's an ease between them, they communicate their needs, they trust each other, they laugh and forgive easily, they want each other to be happy, they have so much love for each other, and they can see a life that they want to create and share together. I can still feel the happiness I felt for Michael in that moment, and gratitude that I got to witness him finding and falling in love with his life partner. Over the years, their beautiful relationship, their balanced and mutual giving, their capacity to be there for each other has inspired me. And in subsequent Fam Dins, David began joining us.

From that dinner onward, I had an inner chant that I shared with Michael—"I want to find my David." I let go of imagining any of my future partner's attributes and focused instead on how I wanted to feel: Seen. Heard. Loved. Held. That my soul had met her match. And that inexplicable *je ne sais quoi* that some couples have. I guess if I had to name it in a word, *magic*. I wanted to feel that something divine was at work between us. That our relationship and our connection to the divine was inextricably linked. Yes, I know. Dream on. But this is what I knew I needed. And this helped me date. Or more like, this meant that I said a whole lot of "No, thank you." I knew how I wanted to feel and this became my standard, my tool of discernment to navigate through the vast and varied dating pool of NYC.

I was given *a lot* of unsolicited dating advice. The fact that I had divorced seemed to hang a placard around my neck that read: *Needs love. Needs help.* I got every comment on the spectrum of advice from "You need to open up, be adventurous, just hook up" to "You need to just stop trying, just forget about meeting someone and then you will."

The search for love in the modern world doesn't have to be bereft of ancient wisdom. In addition to my Disciplined Hope that at some point, I will inevitably meet someone who is divinely aligned for me, I leaned heavily on this passage from the Gospel of Mary Magdalene for guidance:

> "Peace be with you!" he said. "Acquire my peace within yourselves! Be on your guard so that no one deceives you by saying, 'Look over here!' or 'Look over there!' For the child of true Humanity exists within you. Follow it! Those who search for it will find it."[1]

This passage reminds me that the true search for love happens within. There's nowhere I need to go, and there's no app I need to download, or couples workshop I need to attend. The further I go within and meet with that peace that's deep inside me, the closer I am to meeting with love in ways I never have before outside of myself. There's nothing "over there," outside of ourselves. The real work of creating a fulfilling relationship with someone else comes from the depth of our capacity to accept and trust ourselves.

In Christian theology, the term *kenosis* is derived from the Greek word for emptiness. It is the emptying of one's own will and becoming entirely receptive to God's divine will. Instead of getting overwhelmed by the onslaught of conflicting advice from outside sources about how to find love, I decided it was far simpler to just go within. I didn't want to will anything into being without it being aligned with what was actually highest for me. My ego wanted a love in my life right then. Yesterday, even. But I wanted to move differently. I wanted to let my ego sit in the backseat and see where a will more than my own might lead me. I wanted to let my soul be my yenta.

I used my soul as a divine filter when it came to weeding through the dating advice I was being given. If I went within and heard a loud, bold-faced yes to any given bit of advice, I would take it. My mom suggested e-mailing my ladyloves (what I call my girlfriends) and telling them I was ready. My soul gave me a fist pump. So I went for it. Shortly after sending the e-mail, a friend replied that she had found "Mr. Right" for me. Two weeks later, I was on my next blind date. And, yes, his name was David.

He was sitting at the bar with his back to me. I knew it was him. And I already liked him. My heart leapt despite my intention to appear calm and collected. It started to flutter like a hummingbird and I felt self-conscious by the time I sat down on the barstool next to him. I was so nervous I worried I may have broken out in a rash. He smiled. I smiled. Not an inch of awkward. I exhaled.

I was expecting some of those dreaded dead silences during dinner. I mean, yes, we had a mutual friend in common, but that didn't mean we would have anything else to talk about except her. But we did. We were both the ones who fought to try to save our marriages. And when he said that his love for his son is like nothing he had ever experienced, I just stared at him, smiling, and said, "Yes, I know."

There was so much that was "right" about my friend's Mr. Right. He was my age, also an indie parent to a young son. He was smart, funny, and handsome.

We both valued family above all else. He really in many ways was everything I thought I was looking for in a partner. The *only* thing that was missing was that *magic*, the sense that we had been brought together by a force greater than ourselves. Within three months, we knew that what we had was good, but it wasn't what either of us really desired.

For so many of us, dating in our thirties is done at warp speed. We want to get to the heart of things fast. We know ourselves more. We're so much clearer about what we need and the truth of who we are. Some of us have been married, or have been in deeply meaningful relationships that have given us the gift of clarity about what it is we need most in a marriage or life partner. Or we've become clear that a more singular life of devotion to our work or to our art is a priority and not partnership or family.

I knew I needed the Dream. For me, that means the sense of my spirituality being wedded to my relationship— that my connection to the divine was also invited into our couplehood. The love of my life could not be separate from my path of being one with the divine.

I was given a boatload of opportunities to sharpen my resolve into an arrow's tip. But, holy crap, it's crazy making. It's so incredibly hard not to take what's right here already in our lives. It's hard to distinguish what's a Dream, as in what we want most in our lives, from a fantasy, as in what is unattainable. Poet and philosopher Rainer Maria Rilke relates that inertia is not the reason that so many human relationships just keep repeating themselves again and again, without phoenix-type renewal or real change. Rilke believes that "it is shyness before any sort of new, unforeseeable experience with which one does not think oneself able to cope."[2] This is what keeps us from having the courage to not only hope for something new, but to hold out for it. To call it into being. We have to be ready for everything, he advises. We have to exclude nothing, not even the most enigmatic. Only then can we "live the relation to another as something alive" and "draw exhaustively" from our own existence.[3]

The best advice I received came from the least expected person, my PR lady. Our conversation had meandered from PR stuff to how she met her husband, when suddenly she blurted out this gem as if momentarily possessed: "You will meet who you love while doing what you love." Boom. I got those full-body chills and knew it was the truth for me. Shortly after that, I met the High Priestess of Desire for lunch while she was in town for a meeting with her PR lady. And we each knew that it was too much to hold to what we wanted most in our lives, and in our next relationships, on our own. We needed a sisterhood of what's next. We needed to support each other when our Disciplined Hope falters or when we feel derailed by someone who comes into our lives as an almost-but-not-quite right. We needed support in saying no to find our yes. So we decided to imagine, even across the country from each other, that our pinkies were looped in solidarity, faithful to the Dream that we will hold out for who we truly desire.

A few months later I spent New Year's Eve at another friend's apartment in the East Village. I've done this for the past three years since my divorce. I knew from previous years that she has a shoe-free home, so I prepared this year, and arrived wearing knee-high Wonder Woman socks. A miracle maven, she has a tradition of asking everyone at the dinner table to share what miracle we want to manifest most in the New Year. I have a tradition of standing up on my chair to announce what miracle I want to manifest. So this year I stood up, the small red capes on my Wonder Woman socks cascading down my calves, and declared, with my hands on my hips, something like, "I'm just going to anchor into being me. Fully. Completely. I'm just going to stay right here and radiate the love that I am, like a lighthouse. He'll find me."

While working on the book, Lodro and I met and talked about what we would share in this chapter on dating. As I was taking some notes, he covertly created a profile for me on Tinder. As Lodro explained, Tinder is a dating (or a flirting) app for singles looking to connect to people in their immediate area. Of course my knee-jerk response was *no way, that's not me.* But surprise, surprise, when I checked within for a sense of whether it was right for me, my soul was already flirting. (And it was fun, collecting Tinder boos.)

I was swiping left and right, and flirting with men I knew I would never actually go meet, until the day that I swiped my way right up to my former husband's profile! I texted Lodro immediately. Laughing. It kind of knocked the wind out of me, though. So I kept the information of one real connection I made and deleted my short-lived Tinder account. I honed in on my dating maxim: "You will find who you love while doing what you love." And so the night came, up in the Berkshire Mountains, in the middle of January, when I was invited out for a drink with a group of people who worked at the spiritual center where I was leading a REVEAL retreat. I heard a loud, bold-faced yes within. So even though I was tired, I went. The man who was sitting across from me, named David, ordered us both a glass of red wine and when he toasted "to alchemy" we locked eyes. Only time will tell who he is for me. But weeks later when he wrote in an e-mail, "The time has come to never be thirsty again. Hope springs eternal, and it springs from within," I knew I had met "my David."

The Shark of Fixed Expectations

LODRO

> The point I want to make is that love can be true and lasting, under the right conditions . . . Yet often, instead of giving love room to expand, we box it in with our expectations. Expectations make our love conditional on what the other person does or says . . . For love to last, it is best not to have too many expectations. It is better just to offer love.
>
> —The Karmapa, Ogyen Trinley Dorje, *The Heart Is Noble*

My friend Brett works for the U.S. State Department. In the year leading up to his departure overseas he was based in Washington, D.C., taking language classes, and going on a million first dates. Brett's a handsome, charming, well-dressed young diplomat and he met a number of women on online dating sites. They would go out and have a lovely time. That is, until Brett would reveal that after his training he would be stationed for a year plus at the border of Syria and Jordan.

In that moment, the date would unravel. There were conditions on Brett taking a woman on a date that he was a bit naïve about. Brett would be accused of wasting some poor lady's time. These individuals were not looking for an adventure in meeting new people, but were interviewing him for the role of their next life partner. The way Brett explained it, the women he was seeing viewed the hour and a half leading up to this revelation as a pathway to a long-term relationship, if not marriage, starting as soon as they sat down to eat. The fact that he would be gone a year messed with their expectations. The women were disappointed by the fact that he would eventually leave. Brett was disappointed because he was looking to get to know someone, but couldn't find anyone who was content with his situation.

I may be a bit biased, because I know Brett's intentions were good, but I was surprised to hear about the level of fixed expectations that these ladies brought into their first date. They liked the guy they were sitting with, found him charming, and immediately extrapolated that there would be a second date, and another, and another, until they moved in together and continued on the path toward everlasting bliss. There was very little room for enjoying one another's company just to enjoy one another's company. It had to become something more. An experience that could blossom into love began with too many expectations.

While Brett's case may be unique, I know from my own experience, as well as those of my friends, that it's hard to wade too far into the waters of romantic interest before the shark of fixed expectations starts nibbling at your heels. In my relationships, either I've suspended thoughts of "what's going to happen next" or the lady has, but rarely both. After a few good dates I might find myself asking the lady about her family, and later contemplating scenarios within which I win over her dad. Or she might ask if I think kids are in my future, scoping out whether I'm ready to settle down and raise a family. That shark nips at our heels, but only because we have trained it to do so.

I should clarify: I do think it's great to meet someone and aspire to be with them and cherish their company long term. However, if you go into a date with an extremely detailed plan of "what I need to be happy" laid out, there's a lot of room for you to be disappointed. That is boxing yourself in, as the Karmapa points out in the quote that opens this section. The more detailed you are in constructing this "what I need to be happy" list, the more you leave the door open for that shark of fixed expectations to swim right up to you and take a bite. And for many of us, we've left that door wide open for years.

Let me give you an example. You've been through the ringer. You have dated a lot of people that you, in retrospect, should not have dated. You know better now. So you sit down and write a list. The person you want to date should have dark hair. They should have glasses, but don't always need to use them. They should enjoy reading, and *The New York Times* crossword. They should be from the East Coast or Midwest; definitely no West Coasters allowed. They should be interested in your religious beliefs; ideally they should belong to the same religious tradition. They should have a job in government. Or do nonprofit work. They should play an instrument. And have an accent. And be between the ages of 28 and 30.

Now that you have a list you can do what many people do these days, which is go online. I am not opposed to online dating. But I do believe some people look to it in the same way others turn to online shopping. They can browse a selection of human beings like they would a pair of shoes and order one customized to their specifications. The difference between online dating and shoe shopping is that when the mail arrives you often get the shoes described on the website. With online dating you show up at a restaurant and it's a complete crapshoot as to whether the description online was accurate.

More often than not the guy has said things on his profile that were appealing but not actually true. He's never read a book in his life, and although he used to work in nonprofit, now he's all about getting the cash at his high-powered corporate finance job. Or the most common one: he looks nothing like his picture. Let's not underestimate the power of physical attraction here. Or as was the case with Meggan, they end up being your father's doppelgänger. Or they have a Hitler tattoo, which was the case for me. That long list of fixed expectations did not serve you well; the shark swallowed you whole.

Let's give a more charitable example. On paper, your date should be perfect for you. You met him on Match.com and he meets every criterion you listed. He's 29, he's from Boston—but his mom's British so he's got that lovely accent—has great taste in literature, same religious views as you, runs a nonprofit providing musical instruments to orphans, and clearly knows a four-letter word for deep romantic affection. Yet halfway through the date you make a joke and it goes way over his head. Ten minutes later the same thing happens. He walks you to your door, gives you a polite kiss good-bye, and walks off. Nothing bad happened, but you have a sudden realization: This guy doesn't get you. There is no magic, as Meggan discussed, no *je ne sais quoi.*

The thing is, you walked in with your list of what you needed to be happy with another person. It was quite long. And you found someone who you thought met those criteria, only to discover they were not the person you hoped they were. Or they had changed. Or the chemistry was off. Even with your list you couldn't shop your way into the perfect spouse. In my experience, it's simply not possible to do that. When we unleash the shark of fixed expectations we are bound to get eaten.

So why bother? Let's slay the shark and relax our set notions of exactly what we need in a spouse to be happy. I am of the belief that you can't pick who you fall in love with. You could have a long list of what you think it will take for you to be happy, only to be swept off your feet by someone who has zero of those "must-have" qualities on your list. When we drop fixed expectations, we allow love to flourish. As the Karmapa said, "For love to last, it is best not to have too many expectations. It is better just to offer love."

That has always been the case with me. Whenever I have come across a vision for my ideal woman, complete with "what I need to be happy," I meet someone who flies in the face of said list and fall madly for her. The shark retreats and I am able to love freely, without set notions of who the person should be or what the relationship should look like.

In my experience, that is the joy of remaining open to whomever you encounter. If you find someone who complements a certain aspect of who you are at that time, and it seems to work and they get you, I encourage you to lean wholeheartedly into that relationship. There is so much you can get from it.

I remember going through a very difficult period when one of my closest friends died. I met a woman who had gone through a similar experience of losing a friend, and while a multitude of people made a point of telling me it made zero sense for me to date this particular woman, she got me. She understood the grief and the crazy that were raging inside of me, and wouldn't judge me. In that way, it was a therapeutic experience to date her, even though some part of me knew it was not going to work out long term.

While that may be a dramatic example, this woman (and many others I have had the pleasure of loving) opened my heart in a big way. This is the flip side of fixed expectations, known in Buddhism as *bodhicitta*. Bodhicitta is a Sanskrit word. "Bodhi" can be translated as open or awake, and "citta" as heart or mind. It is saying that when we drop fixed mind we can connect to an inherent well of power and joy, an awake heart. We can love fully when we suspend thoughts about the future of a relationship or how we have been hurt in the past. When we are present, we are open.

Suggestions for maintaining an open heart while dating

From Meggan

1. See dating as an adventure in meeting new people, not as an interview for your next life partner.

2. Consider every date, every relationship as an opportunity to discover more of who you are and what you truly desire in a partner.

3. Identify at least one friend or family member who can figuratively "loop pinkies" with you as you date and practice Disciplined Hope to find the person who really matches your desires and needs.

4. Focus on the way you want to feel when you're with this person. And whatever it is that you want this next love to give you, give it to yourself now as much as possible.

5. If you're confused about a potential partner, become aware of how your body feels.

FROM LODRO

1. Don't let your head cloud your heart. Trust your heart, above all else.

2. Don't put the cart before the horse. Just enjoy your time together. Relax.

3. While on your date, just be present with the other person as much as possible.

4. Don't censor yourself. If something comes up, trust that your date will be able to handle it.

5. Have faith. You are inherently good enough, worthy enough, kind and smart enough for anyone you might want to date.

CHAPTER 4

How to Fall in Love Without Losing Yourself

> With true love, you feel complete in yourself; you
> don't need something from outside.
>
> —Thich Nhat Hanh, *Fidelity*

It's Not Called "Strolling into Love"

LODRO

I've always been fascinated with the term "falling in love." We could call it any number of things—stepping into love, strolling into love—but we choose to say falling in love. It's like we have held ourselves so tight, in our little cocoon of being self-involved, that we equate beginning to love another person with throwing ourselves off a cliff; we are falling without any parachute or sense of where we may land. It makes this simple act of opening our heart to others sound dangerous.

In a sense, falling in love *is* dangerous, because it is threatening to the ego. This other person wears away at all the protective layers we have put up around our heart, scrubbing us down to a vulnerable and tender core. We are not used to being this vulnerable around another human being, so it's uncomfortable.

When we are exposed, we know we can easily be hurt. And many of us have been. Repeatedly. I recall an on-again, off-again romance with a med student when I was in my midtwenties. After the millionth time she broke up with me, I was devastated. My friend took me out for lunch and as I sobbed in the quiet restaurant he shot me a look. Overall he was being supportive, but in that inadvertent glance I saw reflected back just how ridiculous I appeared and how silly the whole situation was. What happened not three months later, when I felt whole again? I fell into a loving and supportive relationship that lasted several wonderful years. My story is not uncommon; we often put our heart on the table only to have someone else ignore it or kick it away. Yet what do we do the next time we find someone we want to invite into our life? We fall in love again. We put the heart back on the table.

Alongside the discomfort there can also be excitement. This is our most genuine self, and to have another person see and appreciate that is tremendously rewarding. And while it is rewarding to have this other person in our lives, we are not dependent on them to love. As we have outlined earlier, we can love, independently, on our own. The fact that we bring someone in from the outside world and include him or her in our love is just a huge bonus. But what do we mean when we say "true love"?

From a Buddhist perspective, true love is said to consist of four major qualities:

1. *maitri*, loving-kindness

2. *karuna*, compassion

3. *mudita*, sympathetic joy

4. *upeksha*, equanimity

If you want to love another human being, you know you must start with yourself. These four qualities bridge that transition between loving yourself and loving others to bring about something I would like to call a loving practice. I don't use the term "loving practice" lightly. I think it is a genuine practice to love. It involves us loving others despite knowing that they will leave us, or move away, or die. It involves us loving them as they are, for as long as we can, appreciating them for who they are as opposed to who we wish they would be. Recognizing the impermanence of our situation and seeing the other person with understanding is a true practice. We befriend them. We join with them in both the pains and pleasures of our shared existence. And we open our heart to include all sorts of beings in this regard. Loving practice is a practice we can engage in every day. With that in mind, let's look at these four aspects of loving practice more fully:

Maitri, Loving-Kindness

Maitri comes from the Sanskrit word *mitra*, or friend. In essence we are saying that the root of love for ourselves and others is friendship. You must learn to befriend yourself before even thinking of loving other people. If you are constantly at war with yourself, how do you think you can live peacefully with another? If you cannot love yourself, you cannot love anyone else. The common translation for maitri is "loving-kindness." We are offering a gentle and loving presence. Once you have offered that inwardly, befriending yourself, then you can express this same friendship to another being.

The other year I was on a train from Rome to Florence, as I was taking some time in Europe to write and work on my nonprofit, the Institute for Compassionate Leadership. During the train ride I thought of a woman that my close friend was dating, and I fantasized about their wedding, and the speech I would give, if I were asked to give a speech. Imagining the two of them making this sort of commitment, one I know my friend longs for, I felt my heart opening. Tears of joy came to my eyes.

I had been practicing loving-kindness for myself for days, and also for other people in my life. That loving-kindness practice seeped into this moment, and I felt genuine friendship and well-wishes for this woman I had yet to meet. Based on how things are going right now I am not confident my friend will marry this woman, but just the thought of being able to share in their happiness made me love her almost as much as I love my friend. That is one example of loving-kindness. Through taking the time to befriend myself, I could express this same gentle quality to my friends, and even people I don't know yet.

Karuna, Compassion

As I mentioned, I run the Institute for Compassionate Leadership. It's a training program for individuals who know they want to help the world but aren't entirely clear how they want to go about doing that. We put them through an intense training in meditation, community organizing, and practical leadership skills; get them executive coaching and mentors; and by the end of their time with us, they thankfully come out the other end more openhearted and self-aware. While I'm biased, I believe they become the compassionate leaders this world needs.

Through spending a lot of time meditating, participants in the institute begin to become more aware of their own habitual patterns and how they suffer. Then, as they begin to engage diverse communities as part of their volunteer work, the participants start to notice similarities between their own experience and what others are going through. Yes, the story lines may look different, but at our core we all suffer in similar ways.

Compassion, in this case, is the desire to relieve the suffering of others. The notion of the Sanskrit word *karuna* is that having related to our own suffering we know how scary the darkest parts of our mind can be. We then see others grappling with similar afflictions and our heart goes out to them quite naturally. We have empathy for them. And, thankfully, because we have learned to befriend ourselves, we know how to skillfully help others do the same thing. That is one of the most inspiring parts of each class at the institute—seeing when participants realize they are able to help others because suffering is a universal affliction. We can all be there for each other.

The key here is understanding the other person. The Zen teacher Thich Nhat Hanh wrote, "Understanding is the other name of love. If you don't understand, you can't love."[1] For the institute, that means our participants spend a lot of time learning deep listening and organizing techniques for discovering shared values so that when they encounter people from different backgrounds they can understand how to help and how to love more skillfully.

I was at a bar a few weeks ago and really hit it off with the bartender. He was in his late forties, maybe early fifties, and bragged to me and my friend that he and his wife have been together since they were teenagers.

"What's your secret?" I asked, hoping for some gem of wisdom I could share in this book. Ned the Bartender thought about it for a moment. "Okay, I'll tell you." My friend and I leaned in, in deep anticipation. "We have sex every single day."

"Surely not every single day," my friend replied amicably. Ned got serious. He leaned in, too. "Every. Single. Day."

A few days later my friend and I popped back into the same pub to play some darts. We were in luck that night because in addition to seeing Ned again we met his lovely wife. Once we got her alone I said, "I heard you and Ned have been together since you were in your teens."

"Oh yeah. Long time now," she said.

I asked her the same question: "What's your secret?"

Ned's wife didn't even hesitate with her answer. "Understanding. Space and understanding."

As Thich Nhat Hanh points out, understanding is another way to say love. While I'm sure their awesome sex life was certainly part of their good track record, I am guessing the fact that Ned and his wife offered one another a lot of understanding led to them having a very compassionate (and passionate) relationship.

Mudita, Sympathetic Joy

The flip side of understanding someone else's suffering and wanting to relieve it is sharing in his or her joy. The term *mudita* is sometimes translated as sympathetic joy, or even altruistic joy. It's the delight you have in appreciating your own experience, whatever that experience may be, and sharing that with another. You are there with them when they suffer and when they are happy. It's of course rooted in the fact that you are already comfortable with the times when *you* suffer and when *you* are happy. You are able to weather both on your own, so now you can weather them with another person.

Sometimes sympathetic joy can get muddied by feeling like you possess the other person. To return to Thich Nhat Hanh's teachings, he writes, "Love can bring us happiness and peace as long as we love in such a way that we don't make a net to confine ourselves and others."[2] You may long to just be there and experience the joy of another, but because you get confused and try to pin them down you get in your own way and things get messy.

Sometimes we forget that just because we love someone, it does not mean they are ours to own. The idea of bodhicitta is that our love flows freely, without the need to lock down or possess anyone. We love because we naturally long to love. The other person loves us back, ideally in a similar fashion. That is when things remain playful and fun. That is when sympathetic joy runs wild.

If we return to the analogy of falling in love as falling off a cliff, there are times when we try not to fall so hard. We grab onto rocks jutting out from the mountainside and cling tight for a moment, trying to solidify our position. The way this manifests toward our loved one is in setting up specific things that we think they owe us. We get disappointed that they no longer buy us flowers just because, but only on special occasions. We are angry if they do not call when they usually do. We start fights when their ex e-mails them. In other words, we put up barriers around our heart because falling in love is scary. It's easier to fight and push someone away than it is to accept them openly and without judgment.

When you suspend judgment of the person you are getting to know, and when you allow yourself to feel their joy as your own, you are pushing yourself away from that rock and free-falling. You are connecting with the idea of befriending yourself and others. You are leaning into the deep understanding that is the foundation of every compassionate relationship. With the base of the first three qualities—loving-kindness, compassion, and sympathetic joy—the feeling of falling is suddenly not scary, but liberating. We enjoy the fall, because we see the other person is falling right beside us. We are not alone in this groundless territory. We look our partner in the eye and know that even though we're falling, we're in this together.

Upeksha, Equanimity

Sometimes people think equanimity is a feeling of being completely at peace. However, if you turn to the definition of equanimity in any dictionary, you will discover that it actually means the ability to remain calm in the face of complete uncertainty. It is because you are free-falling that you are able to practice equanimity.

At times the Sanskrit word *upeksha* has been translated not just as "equanimity" but also as "inclusiveness." As Thich Nhat Hanh writes, "When you love one person, it's an opportunity for you to love everyone, all beings."[3] All beings in this case means not just you and your lover. It's your difficult neighbor and the co-worker that annoys you and the man who accidentally took the coffee you ordered. It is truly everyone.

The more we do loving practice the more we drop the dualistic barrier between the one who loves and the one being loved. You realize that all of those individuals suffer and are joyful, just like you. You are no different.

It makes no sense to break the world up into people you like, people you don't like, and people you really couldn't care less about. They are all people. You are a person. We offer our love to "us," and "us" includes everyone.

If you take these four qualities to heart, you will be able to love more fully. I have been working with them for some years and they have changed me tremendously. I fall in love all the time. When I am at my best, I fall in love a half dozen times a day. I know Meggan does, too. We talk about it almost every time we see one another.

I notice after I have been practicing meditation regularly and in longer periods than normal, I walk into the world and feel like my heart can accommodate anything. When I see a playful puppy I fall in love. When I spy a new couple nuzzling against one another on the train I fall in love. When I walk by a group of friends reconnecting I fall in love. When my heart is open I find I am less concentrated on me and my concerns and more available to the world around me. As a result I am exposed to many things every day that I can love wholeheartedly.

One of the people I am very inspired by is His Holiness the 17th Karmapa, Ogyen Trinley Dorje. He has lived a very hard life for someone who is referred to as His Holiness. While a teenager he fled from Chinese pressure in his home country of Tibet into India under extreme duress, only to have the right to his position questioned by political lamas. Now, he is in his early thirties. You might think that having lived through tremendous difficulty he would be tough, but my experience of him is that while he is strong he is tremendously loving. Here are some words of his that touch me deeply:

I want to share with you a feeling I have. I feel that my love does not have to remain within the limitations of my own life or body. I imagine that if I am no longer in the world, my love could still be present. I want to place my love on the moon and let the moon hold my love. Let the moon be the keeper of my love, offering it to everyone just as the moon sends its light to embrace the whole earth.[4]

When we learn to love, we create space for more than just loving ourselves and one other being. We manifest a love that exists way beyond what we conceive of as possible. We manifest a love that can embrace the whole world, where everyone—including the people we like and those we don't and those we don't even know—can experience our love. That is the power of an open heart. That is the power of love.

When you pass away, how do you want to be remembered? I want to be remembered as someone who knew how to love. I know that through loving practice I can have an impact on this earth way beyond what I might physically do in this lifetime. Through loving-kindness, compassion, sympathetic joy, and equanimity I believe I can fall in love with everyone. It won't be scary; it will be liberating. I enjoy falling in love.

Always with a Leg to Stand On

MEGGAN

Common symptoms include: weight loss, sleepless nights, erratic behavior—like laughing one minute and doing the ugly cry the next, or even both at the same time—and all the while feeling like a glowstick radiating a light that everyone in your life comments on, even the mailman and strangers you pass on the street. Nothing looks the same; somehow the quality of your life has been upgraded to high definition. Everything is brighter, and lighter.

When the symptoms worsen, expect everything to seem . . . fun; the mundane is now infused with meaning. Every detail is perceived, every synchronicity acknowledged. A comment is overheard in passing and becomes a divinely timed message. Nothing appears accidental. Everything takes on a numinous quality as if your entire life is being conducted, symphony-like, by this one significant truth: you are in love.

You are in love and it's the most intoxicating paradox. You are invincible, or at least you're aware now of superpowers that before this love were dormant. You feel infused with a confidence that makes you strong, brazen even. You catch yourself looking in the mirror far more often, noticing small nuances about your face that your love has illuminated: the way your eyebrow arches dramatically when you're curious, the way your lips look after several hours of kissing, the way your body feels like a brand-new one—filled with gut lurches and moments of melting in places only a surgeon could reach. You see yourself in a new way, as a miraculous soul in Lululemon yoga gear filled with the love you're so grateful you now get to share.

And at the exact same time, you feel absolutely and utterly vulnerable. You are a mollusk suddenly bereft of its shell. You are a bleating, beating heart and every expression or step you make has the potential to leave you feeling gutted. An unreturned text, an e-mail that no matter how many times you look never appears in your inbox, an unclear tone in your love's voice—all these seemingly small things have the power to derail you and captivate your darkest thoughts for a staggering amount of time. You do whatever you can to try to dim and numb the truth from surfacing, but it's there like a bold-faced chapter title above this time in your life, the truth that you are utterly and entirely *out of control.*

You toss back and forth between fearlessness and fear. So how do you anchor in the vicissitudes of emotion when you're falling in love? Or more precisely, what do you hold on to when you're in a free fall toward love, fully conscious of both your newfound strength and also your palpable vulnerability?

My paternal ancestors, the Wattersons, are from the Isle of Man. So, that makes me Manx. And the Manx flag is of three legs strategically positioned so that no matter how the image is placed, there's always a leg to stand on. My excessive exposure to mystics, mystical texts, and spiritual teachers the world over has given me some truths to hold on to so that when I fall in love I can do so without landing on my face—or at least, not stay face-planted longer than necessary. And I can remain in right relation to the new love in my life as my world gets turned upside down by it.

"Nothing real can be threatened." A Course in Miracles

Love is real. So no matter what, the love you cultivate in this relationship will remain with you. Anchor in the truth that regardless of where this love takes you, your capacity to love has already been exponentially widened. This love, if you let it, already has the power to add more life to your life, no matter the outcome—commitment, long-term partnership, or a more fleeting, cometlike love that blasts a crater-size hole through your heart and lets you love larger for the rest of your life. Anchor in the truth that this love, even at its very beginning stages, has given you the gift of shifting you from where you were before. You may have been epically lonely, or you may have subtly forgotten that you are lovable, and desired. You may have been caught up and even bored with life and this love came in like a wrecking ball to demolish the humdrum so you can rebuild a life that's closer to what you had hoped. This love, whatever it is or turns out to be, is a gift. All it takes is you choosing to see it as this from the very start.

Our model of love has been ruled by some seriously misguided math for far too long. In order for one plus one to equal one in the love relationship, one person has to be subsumed or sacrificed to make the twosome appear "wed" in a sacred union. There's nothing sacred about martyrdom, about silencing one half of a divine duo that should equate to more life, not less. Instead of one plus one adding up to one in the love relationship, I think what so many of us are longing for is a love that allows for one plus one to equal three. Let me explain.

During an exceptionally poignant REDLADIES meeting, we were commenting on the conflicting twin desires of falling madly in love and also remaining alone. One REDLADY in particular shared that she has been alone most of her life because of a deep-rooted belief that if she falls in love she will be consumed by her partner and lose the precious time she has to herself, to her thoughts, and to her dreams. In the course of the conversation, she revealed that her mother was only just now beginning to "reclaim" her life in her midfifties.

And she felt like some part of her vowed as a little girl to never lose herself to begin with, which then on an unconscious level has forced her to sabotage any potential long-term relationship because it equated to the loss of her true self. And even though she had grown lonely, and felt unchallenged by her single status, she preferred loneliness to getting eclipsed.

As much as the romantic in me swoons at the idea of becoming one with someone else, and as much as a total eclipse of the heart sounds awesome in theory (and on the dance floor of the bar/bat mitzvahs I attended as a teen), it's just not real. Two individuals joining to become one individual is not realistic. It doesn't work. And that's why when one partner is allowing her- or himself to be overshadowed by the other, letting more and more of their soul's real needs be usurped and undervalued in the relationship, eventually that relationship will die.

Love doesn't ask for a subtraction or a negation of who we are. If that's what you're feeling or experiencing in a love relationship, it's important to question whether this "love" is more about fear. Love asks us to be all of who we are. Love asks us to let go of the egotistical limits we've placed on our lives and become more, not less. Rather than having a limiting belief that love holds the power to eclipse the true self, I believe love is best represented by the image of the vesica piscis:

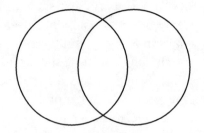

The vesica piscis is an ancient symbol of sacred geometry that is linked to Christian mysticism and Kabbalah. The two circles share the same radius in such a way that the center of each circle lies on the perimeter of the other. The wisdom of this image suggests that when two individuals come together a third is created. Each circle maintains its own integrity. And yet, they overlap in a way that the vesica piscis, the egg-shaped circle in the middle, is created. One plus one equals three. This can only be possible, though, if each remains true to themselves—if they maintain their own boundaries by being honest about the desires and needs that cannot be compromised. I will reveal more about the alchemy of the vesica piscis as it relates to the sacred marriage in Chapter 5, but for now it represents a powerful ideal to hold to when you're falling in love or resisting falling in love for fear of losing yourself.

The metaphysical text *A Course in Miracles* relates that "nothing real can be threatened." So the love you create in this relationship cannot be threatened (even if the relationship ends), and the love of your unique soul cannot be threatened because it is yours alone and you honor it by voicing your needs and desires throughout the relationship. Love so often comes in and illuminates what is actually real for us, which can be shocking and disorienting. Those fictions we have believed about ourselves for most of our lives get challenged. And this can feel uncomfortable at best, terrifying at worst. But the function of love is to expose that numinous core of who we are. It's meant to burn away what isn't real. So as I fall truly, madly, deeply in love with another person, I hold tight to trusting that what is real will remain. No matter how this love unfolds, the truth of who I really am endures.

"The capacity to be alone is the capacity to love."
Osho

Those twinned and seemingly disparate desires that
surfaced in our REDLADIES meeting of wanting to fall
deeply in love and also wanting to remain alone capti-
vated me. It felt like a paradox that was alive and well
within me, and one I wanted to reconcile because it created this conflict. There was a tug-of-war at the core of
my being every time a potential partner arrived. And
also, I was attracting partners that acted out that inner
struggle by showing affection for me that went from hot
to cold at whiplash speeds. I knew I wouldn't meet with
someone who could be unequivocal about their feelings
for me (my deepest desire) if I didn't find a way to resolve
this wrestling match inside me over being in love versus
being alone. Mystic and spiritual author Osho suggests
that "the capacity to be alone is the capacity to love."[5]
Being able to love relies on our ability to be alone. The
two are actually so crucial for the existence of the other
that if we are not able to be alone we are not actually in
love or capable of loving.

At the three-month mark of my relationship with
the man who would ultimately become my husband,
we got in a tremendous fight. (It basically boiled down
to our respective fears—I was afraid he wasn't capable
of loving me, and he was afraid that I wasn't capable of
hearing him.) He decided that this relationship wasn't
right for him, and he broke up with me. Distraught over
losing him, I sobbed so hard I passed out. (I'm laughing about this now because of the soap-opera sound
to it, but in the moment it was pretty scary for both of
us.) What I didn't realize at the time was that I was dependent on the relationship. My inability to maintain

equilibrium at even the idea of him leaving me was a huge indication that my relation to him was unbalanced, and consequently, unhealthy. It felt as though my stability came from him or from our relationship even though on a very real and deep level I knew that it didn't. I kept allowing myself to slide into this imbalanced and antiquated idea that my "wholeness" or sense of fulfillment was dependent on finding the "love of my life." And in a way, it was. It's just that "the love of my life" was within.

When we got back together, and then in a few months broke up again, I felt trapped. I had a recurring dream in which my partner kept locking me in the attic. And only he had the key. I felt so confined. All I wanted was out. And yet, in my waking moments, I fought like an underweight champion to hold our relationship—and eventually, our marriage—together. I was not maintaining the separate and essential circumference of my own circle, my own self. I had become dependent on this love, and even more, addicted to it.

Only if I can be alone within the relationship—meaning at peace with the knowledge that I am whole on my own, I am entire and complete, a world unto myself—can I truly love. My partner isn't an object, a possession, a thing I cannot do without. I might not want to be without him, but I maintain the truth that my happiness is not dependent on him. I'm free. This is the difference between interdependence and codependence. In an interdependent relationship, true freedom—or as Osho calls it, "absolute freedom"—is created. How? When both individuals can maintain the truth that they are enhanced and enlarged by each other and not saved or completed, "they allow the other absolute freedom, because they know that if the other leaves, they will be as happy as they are now. Their happiness cannot be taken by the other, because it is not given by the other."[6] When we know this, and hold true to this, we have no need to "net" or confine our love as Lodro related. Love doesn't confine. It expands. We have never needed to make a choice between honoring our true self, which for most of us is easiest when we're alone, and falling madly in love. We can do both. In fact, in order to love, we have to.

"To love another person is to see the face of God."
Victor Hugo

My mom displays her emotions without reservation and with gusto. I inherited her emotional transparency. And when you put the two of us next to each other, our emotional displays can reach epic proportions. Case in point: Remember that scene from the movie *Indiana Jones and the Temple of Doom* when the "Kali Ma" cult leader is reaching in to tear out the heart of that poor man trapped in an iron cage wearing little more than a turban? My mom and I screamed so loudly and for so long (while clasping hands, no less) that we were actually kicked out of the movie theater.

Years later, and demonstrating an emotion on the opposite end of the continuum, my mom and I bawled with such abandon while sitting in the audience at a performance of *Les Misérables* that the ushers approached us and asked for us to kindly keep it together. The line that set us off, and would continue to set us off every time we heard the soundtrack, was paired with the crescendo of the song, and struck me as an ultimate truth: "To love another person is to see the face of God."

I cried because this validated my experience of love. Love, for me, really has nothing to do with the ego. This is part of why, as Lodro relates, it can feel so dangerous and terrifying to fall in love. Love undresses the ego. Love disarms and displaces the ego. Is who we love really a choice? So far, love for me has come uncontrived and sometimes unbidden. I have felt immensely impotent to love those that my small-me, or my rational mind, or my ego-self is eagerly pushing me to love, people who it would make a whole lot of sense to love. But love has nothing to do with pragmatism. There's something so divine about who we fall in love with precisely because it's out of our control.

And if loving someone cannot be contrived, if we can't "fake" our love for someone, then the reverse must also be true. We cannot convince our partner of their love for us. We do not earn their love, for example, by becoming who we think they want us to be. Love is a gift that goes both ways. Love is inherently reciprocal. Love is innate between two people. It's either there or it isn't. Of course it has to be made, and remade, again and again. It has to be nurtured, respected, and cherished. But the miracle of love is that in a very real way it's beyond our conscious volition. We love, often and hard, those we wished we didn't. We often unintentionally fall for people who are so far from the list of what we thought we wanted that it takes epic thunderbolts to finally get us to realize that love is a force that both exists within us and is far, far larger than any one of our individual lives.

Often when we're falling in love, we labor over explaining ourselves to the other. Or we overextend ourselves to prove or demonstrate that we are worthy of the love they're giving us. I fall more easily and with far more grace when I keep reminding myself that love is not deserved. I can never earn or prove that I am worthy of it. I simply am. My worthiness of love has nothing to do with this other person. It is my birthright. So what I can hold to, and stay grounded in as the ground falls out from beneath me, is the profound gratitude I have to get to love at all. The fact that someone I can love has come into my life is proof alone of the divine. And as the uncertainties and scary ego dismantling take place in the course of my free fall into love, I can breathe deep in the equanimity and tranquility of knowing that this is enough already. The fact that I can love this other person is holy enough, and I am worthy of such proximity to God.

Suggestions for Falling In Love

FROM LODRO

You don't need a partner to place your love upon. As we described, you can simply fall in love. Here is a meditation practice to develop loving-kindness:

After engaging in five or more minutes of shamatha meditation, bring to mind a simple phrase: *May I enjoy happiness and be free from suffering.* Set a timer for two minutes. Repeat that phrase silently to yourself during that time. A wide variety of reactions may occur, from the emotional to the intellectual. Keep bringing your mind back to that phrase, just as you come back to the breath in the shamatha practice. Let the phrase wash over you like a wave and see what comes up in response. See if you have any resistance to offering yourself loving-kindness in this way.

After those two minutes set your timer once more, but this time turn your mind to the image or the name of someone you love dearly. Inserting their name into this contemplation, bring your mind to *May _____ enjoy happiness and be free from suffering.* What would happiness look like for your mother, or best friend, or romantic partner? How are they suffering, and what would change for them if they did not suffer in that way? Once more, when you get distracted and, for example, start thinking of what you want to eat for dinner later, just come back to the phrase you are contemplating.

Next, set your timer and turn your attention to a colleague or friend for whom you feel affection. You can think of what they normally wear, or envision their face, or hold their name in mind. Make this same aspiration for them: *May _____ enjoy happiness and be free from suffering.* What would it take for this person to be happy?

Now we get into tricky territory. Set your timer once more and think of someone who you don't know as well. If your life were a movie they would be an extra in the background. It could be that person you see on your commute every morning or your neighbor down the hall. Even if you don't know their name bring their image to mind and contemplate, *May they enjoy happiness and be free of suffering.*

Our last individual is the difficult person in your life. Even if it's your ex who broke your heart or that jerk at the office, we can still make this aspiration for them, if even just for two minutes. *May _____ enjoy happiness and be free from suffering.* Try not to get lost in the story line around why this person is so difficult; instead aspire that they suffer less and find some form of happiness.

Now we bring to mind all five of these people—you, your cherished one, your friend or colleague, the person who just sort of exists in your life, and your difficult person—and make this aspiration to the group as a whole. *May we all enjoy happiness and be free from suffering.* Expand this aspiration to include everyone on your block, in your neighborhood, your city, state, country, and keep expanding until you make that aspiration for everyone. *May all beings enjoy happiness and be free from suffering.*

Finally, drop the words you have been contemplating. Drop the image you have in your mind. Look up at the horizon. Rest with whatever feelings of love that have come forth.

FROM MEGGAN

I was recently asked to offer the soul-voice meditation for a relationship expert at a weekend retreat she was leading in NYC. I was inspired by the experience because it reminded me how crucial a contemplative practice is, especially when falling in love. *Going within* is a phrase I use often. In the context of this soul-voice meditation, it refers to focusing all our attention on the heart. "The heart" can refer to the odd-looking organ that makes life possible. It can refer to an interior space that only our imagination can fully conjure. Or it can be an intermediary space within our small, human lives where we can encounter what's divine, and far more than us alone.

When we are falling in love, it's so easy to fall out of alignment with our own source of love. We start to forget and eventually believe that this new love in our life is our primary source of love, that we're dependent on that love for our "happily ever after." We forget that a limitless source of love exists within, and so is always within reach, no matter who enters our lives and who leaves. The love of our life, "the one" we are truly meant to meet, is right here just waiting for us to be brave enough to feel how much the heart contains.

The soul-voice meditation is a powerful tool for staying rooted in your own love as you fall in love with someone else. For me, when I enter that mystical space called heart, I feel a sense of encountering my own soul. (As ultimately ineffable as that encounter is.) And in encountering the presence of my own soul, I experience a love that is beyond love. It's unconditional and it's limitless. Exercising the capacity to fill my own heart with the presence of love allows me to stay in right relation to this lover or beloved I've found.

I panic less, and I feel far more equanimity as I fall head over heels for this other person because the practice helps me never forget that this new love is adding more love to my already full heart. This new love can never threaten or disconnect me from an abundant source of love that I have access to within me all the time.

At the relationship workshop, I shared the bare bones of the soul-voice meditation, which is derived from a contemplative practice by the early Christian monastics in the 4th century known as the Hesychasts. Hesychasm is derived from the Greek word *hesychia*, meaning stillness or silence. The aim of the Hesychast was to go within the heart and reach a state of union with the divine. They practiced by curling forward to direct all of their attention and focus into the heart. I tried this practice myself while in seminary. But my body protested—it gave me a sore back and stiff neck. I also wanted to try this meditation not just while I was sitting next to a lit candle before the little altar in my apartment, but also while sitting in a packed, stalled subway car, while encountering a new acquaintance or someone asking for help, or while having a serious conversation with a friend or lover. These were the moments when I most needed the stillness of the love I found through meditation.

I wanted to be able to make a spiritual practice out of meeting with the love that found me effortlessly when all the conditions were optimal, in the least optimal times and places. So, for example, when I was on a pilgrimage to the sacred sites of the Black Madonna and Mary Magdalene after divinity school, I was often "kneed" by the love that would come and overwhelm all other thoughts or feelings in me. All of my time, though, and all of my focus could be on love. I was a pilgrim. That's what we do. We walk to pilgrimage sites and we fall to our knees in love with the divine. What I wanted was to be able to meet with that love no matter where I was, or who I was with or without. So that, for example, while I was transitioning out of my marriage, and taking care of my one-year-old son, I used the soul-voice meditation like a scuba diver uses an oxygen mask. All it takes, seriously, is this:

1. You can be anywhere, seated or standing, or even on the elliptical machine at the gym. The most important thing is that you go within. Drop your awareness into the center of yourself, to what we all refer to as the heart. See it in any way you want—as a red chamber with lit candles, a dance floor with a disco ball, or a field of wildflowers. It doesn't matter the space you imagine; it only matters that you feel that it's your heart—the center of who you are—and that everything is possible here.

2. Set the intention of connecting to the love your soul contains. Or if asking questions feels engaging for you, ask this of your soul: How can I hear you more clearly? Or, if you're more sensate than auditory, ask this: How can I feel you more fully?

3. Give gratitude for whatever information or feelings greeted you (whether you heard what you wanted to hear or felt anything, or not). What I have found is that the more I showed up, and went within, the more consistently I met with the love that exists there. And that if I didn't receive the answer then, I would within the course of the next several days.

For the full soul-voice meditation produced by Hay House, go to my website's home page and receive the free audio at www.megganwatterson.com.

CHAPTER 5

HOW TO COMMIT TO LOVE

> All my life, in nameless, indeterminate ways, I'd
> tried to complete myself with someone else . . . and I
> didn't want that anymore. I wanted to belong to myself.

— Sue Monk Kidd, *The Mermaid Chair*

Semper Fidelis

MEGGAN

It was one of those movies I didn't just watch; I entered into it. The dreamlike quality of the scenes, the fleeting nature of them, and the rich symbolism—the medieval tapestries of *The Lady and the Unicorn*, an inner courtyard, a pilgrimage to an ancient monastery in France called St. Michel—sent an invitation to my unconscious. I could feel that, like a great big fish making its way up from the depths, there was something tremendous that the movie *To the Wonder* was about to reveal to me.

I identified of course with the passionate and somewhat ephemeral French woman (also an indie mom) in the film who falls in love with the down-to-earth American man. I was riveted by their love story, their struggle to commit to their love once he transplants the two of them to his hometown in Middle America. And just as equally, I was riveted by the love story of the local priest, and the private struggle he endures to remain committed to his vows to God. Why? I want both. I am both. I want the human, passionate love partner and I want that devoted, all-consuming love of the divine. By the end of the movie I realized there was a part of me that has always struggled with this dichotomy. How can I be committed to one person and also committed to my relationship with the divine?

For me, revelation looks something like a sob-fest. I bawl my eyes out when I finally encounter something that I've been living out unconsciously for years. I was grateful I was watching the movie alone. I held nothing back. And because I had rented it on demand, I could re-wind and listen to Javier Bardem's lines again and again. He plays the part of the priest. I'll refrain from gushing about just how hot he looks in priestly garb. (For now.) It's a moment in the movie when the two love stories intersect. He, the priest, is giving a sermon about love, and the couple struggling to stay married is sitting in the back pew listening. As soon as he starts the sermon, my cheeks flush. He commands, "You shall love." In other words, whether we like it or not, we are inevitably, inexorably going to love. He explains that ultimately love isn't an emotion, or a feeling. Love is a divine presence within us that we have the power to awaken. It's a presence that doesn't change and shift like cloud formations. It's eternal. He ends the sermon by asking us to know each other in "that love that never changes."

Committed relationships come in many forms: Family. Friends. Lovers. Partners. They come in every possible combination of people of every sex, gender, size, race, class, age, economic reality, and . . . fashion sense. Love does not divide. Love is what unifies. Yet, I rarely felt undivided when I was in love and in a committed relationship. I felt split between my desires for a human love and my desires for union with the divine. *To the Wonder* gave me a better understanding why.

The dominant cultural models present human love and spiritual devotion as two separate worlds and realities—as two irreconcilable commitments. There is falling in love and committing (through the institution of marriage) to a single human person, and then there is being devoted to and committing your life (through the institution of religion) to the divine. I can say with all honesty that what has mattered most to me is that I find a partner I can share my life with—both the blissful and the straight-up sucky bits. And also, from my earliest memories, I have literally swooned at the love I find from within—a love that is more than love, a divine love that leaves me wanting for nothing. The taste of that union is authentically my one true desire. After hearing the priest's sermon in *To the Wonder*, I realized that I couldn't fully commit to one person if it meant sacrificing my commitment to the divine. What I needed was a union of irreconcilables.

Semper fidelis is a Latin phrase that means "always faithful." I have never struggled with faith in the power of human love or with faith in the presence and reality of the divine. What I have struggled with is how to remain semper fidelis to both. Let's go back to Javier Bardem in his smoking-hot (and slightly too tight) priestly outfit. His sermon, which I have since used while officiating several wedding ceremonies, relates a way to reconcile these desires to be faithful both to a human love and to the love of the divine—especially his command to awaken to the divine presence in each of us, and to know each other from that place that never changes. This is the way those seemingly disparate commitments align as one: my path in a committed relationship with another soul is to never abandon or betray my commitment to the voice of my own soul.

Like Lodro's (as you'll see), my most significant committed relationship ended not because of some blatant or dramatic betrayal. After therapy, workshops, and many late-night talks over the course of a year, my partner decided our relationship just wasn't right for him. He filed for divorce under "irreconcilable differences." I found out in this relationship that I'm a fighter. I found out that I believe "the one" is a choice we make within our hearts (daily), not some predestined truth outside of us and outside of time. I found out just how much I want someone who can be fully committed with me in a relationship, or two feet in, as I like to refer to it. I found out I need a partner who lives as intensely as I do—with intention, passion, and presence.

And I also found out that although I went within and heeded the voice of my soul about major choices in our relationship—when he asked me to marry him, when he asked me about conceiving our son, and when he asked to separate—on a day-to-day basis, I was more concerned with making sure his needs were met, so I forgot about my own. I feared losing his love so much, I was willing to forsake my own love for myself. So it wasn't one major betrayal between us that ended our marriage; it was the unassuming, everyday betrayals that took place within me that made a committed relationship untenable. It was not his inability to be there for me, or his ambiguities about his love for me, that I kept focusing on as "the issues." It was my inability to be there for myself. It was also incertitude and a lack of commitment to my own soul.

There's a passage in the Gospel of Mary Magdalene, when the voice of the soul speaks directly. Mary is recounting to the disciples a vision she had of Jesus where he revealed to her the process of the soul's ascent to God. She relates the various powers that seek to keep the soul bound to this world; Desire is one of them. (This is earthly desire, the ego's desire, which is distinct from the soul's will.) Desire and the soul have a dialogue. And at one point the soul says to Desire, "I saw you. You did not see me nor did you know me. You mistook the garment I wore for my true self. And you did not recognize me."[1] When I first read this passage it sent chills through me. It felt as if my own soul could say the exact same revelation to me—"I saw you . . . and you did not recognize me." The presence of the soul can often feel elusive, if not nonexistent. When we are attached to the ego's desired outcome in a love relationship, it's very difficult to see and to recognize the presence of our soul.

I have never made it through a wedding without tearing up from the sheer bravado and beauty of two people vowing to share their lives together. I have also never made it through a wedding without being in utter awe that this couple is marrying in plain sight of the statistics that they have a fifty-fifty chance of staying together. I often wonder what would happen if in the ceremony the vows weren't just about a union between two souls, but also about remaining faithful to the voice of our own soul. What if we were asked in a committed relationship to cultivate our capacity to love both ways?

Let's return to the sacred geometry of the vesica piscis, those two clearly defined circles that overlap to create a third (an egg-shaped oval). It's a visual of the hopeful ideal that two become three and not one when they come together as two wholes, two indivisible universes, each with a purpose and a powerful reason for being here. The vesica piscis becomes a sacred container, a possibility of being for each of the two lovers to actually become more of who they are as they seek to align their lives together into a single shared life.

Hieros gamos is a Greek term that refers to the sacred marriage of a human being and the divine. The term goes back nearly five thousand years to ancient Sumerian culture, and took form in a fertility ritual. The ritual typically involved these three primary relationships: between god and goddess, between goddess and her priest-king, and between god and his priestess. And the ritual always included these components: a procession, an exchange of gifts, a purification of the beloved couple, a feast, and the consummation of their love in the wedding chamber. The hieros gamos is meant for twin souls, or soul mates. But here's the thing: it has been externalized as the wedding ceremony that takes place between two individuals. It's a ritual, though, that is meant to reflect an inner union, that of our humanity to our own divinity. It's the reuniting of the self and the soul. It's a ritual that suggests we wed that highest aspect within us, "that love that never changes."

I would give a spiritual makeover to the term soul mates—it is a couple vowing fidelity to their own souls, then, where their two souls align and overlap with authenticity; a sacred distance is created, space enough for each of them to become more than they could be on their own. As couples therapist Esther Perel suggests, "Everyone should cultivate a secret garden."[2] It's actually our capacity to cultivate our separateness—and the ability to tolerate the insecurity in a relationship that distance creates—that allows us to be in a committed relationship without sacrificing our sacred vows to our own soul. We can then experience that freedom we all long to feel—the freedom of being entirely ourselves in the presence of another, which comes from our partner witnessing the truth of who we are.

A committed relationship gives us the opportunity to not only cultivate our capacity to love someone else, but also, and just as significantly, it gives us the sustained safety to explore our capacity to love ourselves. The Sufi mystic Rumi says that "Lovers don't finally meet somewhere. They are in each other all along."[3] Meaning, to find someone beloved to us we must become beloved ourselves. How can we expect to have a committed relationship with another if we are not committed to the most integral and authentic aspect of our own being? In his book *Loveability*, psychologist Dr. Robert Holden suggests that "Seen rightly, 'How do I love myself?' and 'How do I love others?' are really the same question."[4] In a way, we try out our love of ourselves on others. We project onto them those aspects of us that we haven't learned yet to fully see, claim, or love. And ultimately what we want is for the love of the other to not sustain us, but rather to be a reflection of our own love for ourselves. We seek to source our own love from within.

I'll admit I swooned when I first saw that elevator scene in the film *Jerry Maguire*, when Renée Zellweger's character translates for Tom Cruise's character what the two lovers sign to each other: "You complete me." But in real life, that concept feels awkward and awful. If someone else completes me, then I am dependent on that other. My sense of self, and wholeness, is inextricably linked to them. How crazy uncomfortable, and how disempowering. And, fortunately, how untrue.

William of Ockham, unlike many theologians of the Middle Ages, did not believe that God could be proved with logical arguments. Theology was a matter of faith and revelation. I feel the same way about love. Love is an adventure between two souls who have vowed to obey their own soul. Which, as Lodro will point out, can be excruciatingly uncomfortable at times—trusting that the one you love will come back to you as they go off from time to time to answer the call of their own soul. The hottest space is the one in between—not a place of merging and "being one," where one person completes the lack in the other's life, but a succulent interdependence, a place of each holding their own holy ground. A meeting of Rabbi Martin Buber's concepts of "I" and "Thou," of two worlds beholding each other from a distance they both desire to cross.

When I commit to love again, it will be a commitment to remain faithful to the voice of love within me, to stay connected to the presence and sacred desires of my own soul. To remain firmly behind my own eyes, anchored in who I am, even as I seek to know my partner and the presence I witness in his gaze. I will remain my own. I will love myself as passionately as I will seek to love him. Dr. Robert Holden suggests that "To love somebody is a commitment that says, 'I will not forget who you are,' and 'I will not abandon you,' and 'Together, we will remember what is real.'"[5] I agree. This is what I want to offer someone else in our love, but only while also remaining semper fidelis to these three vows to my own soul.

Relationships Are Tough

LODRO

Relationships are tough, man. I had a conversation about relationships the other day with my dear friend Susan Piver. Susan is a Shambhala Buddhist teacher and has written a number of books on this topic, including *The Wisdom of a Broken Heart*. She posited a basic truth that I have found meshes with my own experience, and Meggan's. It might mesh with yours, too: relationships are uncomfortable. We sometimes romanticize them, but underlying the good times we had with that past partner there was always some basic discomfort. And if you're in a relationship right now I bet you've experienced some uncomfortable moments there, too.

Let me step back and highlight the first thing the Buddha ever taught: suffering. I have seen numerous translations of the first of the Four Noble Truths that he offered in his initial sermon. The Sanskrit term *dukkha* has been translated as "suffering," and often within the context of "Suffering exists," "Life is suffering," or "There is suffering"; there are even times I have seen the word *suffering* swapped out for *unsatisfactoriness* or *anxiety*. The Buddha, or Awakened One, was awake to the basic notion that no matter what, there is an undercurrent of suffering that exists. That is the nature of reality. There are three types of suffering the Buddha discussed.

The Suffering of Suffering

This is the type of suffering that is part of our human condition: birth, aging, sickness, and death. When we are born it's uncomfortable; we cry because we are disoriented. Then we age and go through awkward growth spurts and our bodies change dramatically in our teenage years. Then we age some more and begin to have experiences where we are physically unable to do what we used to do, and that is painful for us. Along the way we get sick, either in little bursts or for long periods of time, in all sorts of ways. And at the end of it all is death, which is a scary thing to face. Hence, suffering.

Similarly there are the times a relationship gets sick; someone cheats or does something else remarkably disrespectful and the connection is weakened. Then there is death; either the physical death of a loved one or a breakup of some kind. These things are part of the reality of being in relationships just as they are a part of life.

The Suffering of Change

When I talk about suffering, I don't want to make it seem like Buddhists are entirely nihilistic. Ice cream tastes good. You can enjoy eating ice cream. But at a certain point your spoon hits the bottom of the bowl and there's nothing left to eat. You are hurt because your pleasure has come to an end. This truth of impermanence extends well beyond ice cream to our careers, our relationships, and our loved ones.

All-Pervasive Suffering

Because we are changing, and our partner is changing, it's a bit of a dance to stay connected as the whole world moves around us. Often we rub against each other in the wrong way and our delusions of our partner being the perfect person for us is revealed as just that: a delusion. The Zen master Thich Nhat Hanh wrote, "To commit to another person is to embark on a very adventurous journey. There is no one 'right person' who will make it easier."[6] No matter who we choose to accompany us on this journey, it is going to involve discomfort and pain.

The Second Noble Truth the Buddha taught is that there is a reason we suffer: we are ignorant to the nature of reality. We think we can buck the system and find everlasting happiness in the midst of the ever-changing vicissitudes of life. We constantly crave something solid, something permanent, something that will fulfill us, existing *out there* as opposed to *in here*.

The Third Noble Truth is the good news truth: there can be a cessation to suffering. And the Fourth Noble Truth is that there is a path that the Buddha highlighted so you can stop suffering: the Eightfold Noble Path and a slew of teachings on mindfulness and awareness that can be applied to your daily life so you can live a more awake existence.

I mention all of this because these truths play out all the time in long-term relationships. These are not particularly religious truths; they are just how things happen to occur. To return to what my friend Susan pointed out, the truth of relationships is that they are uncomfortable. We suffer in a myriad of ways within them, always trying to seek solid ground and manipulate ourselves or our partner in a way that will "fix" things between us. Even in our most stable of times we think, *Well, it would be nice if they folded the laundry more. Maybe I can let it sit in the dryer until they figure out they need to do that.* It's a weird form of suffering, but if you're like me, you've been there.

Why do we suffer within relationships? Because of the Second Noble Truth: we are ignorant to how we constantly crave something other than what is going on right now. If you are single you might crave meeting "the one." If you're in a relationship you might crave that your illusion of stability goes on forever. If you're going through a breakup or a divorce or have lost your partner to death, you might crave that things ended differently. Craving is an omnipresent aspect of long-term relationships. I know that when I am in a committed relationship I don't always rest with the perceived comfort of having someone to be with. I am drawn to thinking through what our next step might be: *We should take a trip together. I should meet her parents. When is it appropriate for us to move in together?*

Like Meggan, I am the "jump in with both feet" type, and either I encounter the same in a woman, in which case things go quickly and (occasionally) messily, or I encounter the slow-and-steady type and find myself pushing the gas or brakes based on the messages I receive from my partner. Neither of these situations is particularly comfortable, and it's because I am craving something other than what is going on right now that makes it so.

When we crave, we often crave specific outcomes. We have ideas of what it means to be happy. If this person does this sort of thing for me, exactly when I want it, then I will be content. Then, to return to the *Jerry Maguire* example, I will have found someone who completes me. But that's not how contentment works. We often end up discontent because we are constantly disappointed that our idea of what should have happened didn't happen as planned—the timing was off, or it went differently than we wanted.

Thich Nhat Hanh wrote of committed relationships, "When you live with the person twenty-four hours a day, you begin to discover the reality of the other person doesn't quite correspond with the image you have of him or her."[7] As discussed in previous chapters, the more you box yourself in with fixed expectations, the more you will be dissatisfied.

The more images you cling to for your lover, the more pain you bring on yourself.

The alternative to losing ourselves in craving is to relax with the other person, as they are—to accept them, moment by moment. It is acknowledging suffering and saying, *I'm going to love in spite of whatever pain may arise.* I once heard that Chögyam Trungpa Rinpoche responded to a question about the Buddhist idea of karma by saying, "Everything is predetermined . . . until now." In other words, when you are in a relationship with someone you have a certain habitual way of doing things. You carry certain baggage and have certain cravings for particular outcomes. You have a wave of habitual energy propelling you forward to repeat the same mistakes you have made in previous relationships.

For me, I walk into relationships with baggage, including that large duffel bag called "My fiancée left." I thought I would no longer face discomfort in my romantic life because I had found someone who truly got me, who couldn't imagine her life without me, and who cherished me without limit. Until one day she didn't really get me, she could imagine her life without me, and she hit her limit. It was one of those breakups where it's not easily explained. It's not like one of us cheated on the other or we got into a terrific fight due to opposite visions for our shared future. She just got to a point where it no longer felt right for her to marry me, and things fell apart from there.

So going into new relationships, I'm aware that I crave a level of solidity and hope for permanence, while simultaneously fearing that my partner will leave me out of the blue. One might think that everything is predetermined for me to struggle against just being with that person.

But instead I can give up the predetermined sense of struggle I carry; I can relax and appreciate the other person for who they are, and where we are, in a given moment. As Javier Bardem says in *To the Wonder*, right now I can awaken to the divine presence within my partner and myself, and connect with that person in the space of the innate love that never changes. I can wake up and enjoy what's happening right now.

Which brings us again to the Third Noble Truth, the good news: you can stop suffering so much. In the context of a long-term relationship, that looks like becoming present and mindful enough to engage your partner in an openhearted way. You let go of the struggle you perpetuate, notice that your partner is a fluid and changing person, and relax in the midst of that transformation you are going through together.

The Fourth Noble Truth is learning to live with your partner, with all beings really, with complete openness. You acknowledge the suffering and discomfort that arises in your day-to-day existence, and by looking directly at it you see your way through. You stop perpetuating your inner struggle. His Holiness the Karmapa drew a line in the sand on this topic when he wrote, "When you truly love someone, they are extremely precious to you—as valuable to you as your own life. You cherish them even more than yourself. But when you are attached to people, you see them as existing in your life to fill your needs or to make you happy."[8]

If everything is predetermined until now, you can make a choice, in this moment, as to how you want to exist in a long-term relationship. Do you want to use your partner as a way to fill your needs? Or do you want to let love flow, cherishing whatever time you have with them?

If you are able to relax and appreciate the other person, without craving set things from them, then you are building something beautiful. You are building a home. You are creating a safe space wherein your love can flourish. It only exists moment by moment, but it is a true home. Thich Nhat Hanh writes, "If we're practicing mindfulness, there doesn't have to be a conflict between the true home inside us and the true home we make with our partner."[9] With a foundation of self-love we can love someone fully, as they are, without attaching strict conditions on what they must do to deserve our love. We can build a home of our love, facing whatever discomfort arises, shoulder to shoulder.

Suggestions for cultivating sacred space in committed relationships

FROM MEGGAN

1. Identify the activities that allow you to feel connected to the presence of your soul, whether it's long walks, meditating, writing, Rollerblading, or baking. Give yourself the chance to do at least one of these activities once a week.

2. Find a spiritual practice that allows you to really hear your own truth, or what I refer to as the soul-voice. Having a spiritual practice that lets you remain faithful to your own truth is fundamental to creating that space needed to keep the relationship mutually beneficial.

3. Rituals work powerful magic. Marry your own soul. Create a ritual for you to wed the highest aspect of you.

FROM LODRO

1. Find specific activities that you can do together. These can be intimate, such as reading a story to one another before bed, or mundane, such as sharing a favorite TV show you will never ever watch without one another, or extreme, such as bungee jumping.

2. Discuss your spiritual intentions together. Whatever your closely held values, please share them with your loved one. Do not be shy about these intimate aspects of your being. Let your partner get to know you through them.

3. Go away together. Traveling with someone is an excellent way to deepen intimacy, for better or worse. As you continue to deepen your ability to love yourself, take your partner along for the journey—both figuratively and literally.

CHAPTER 6

How to Love Your Friends

Even before I met you I was far from indifferent to you.

—Gwendolen, *The Importance of Being Earnest*

The Boundless Potential for Love

Lodro

I'll share something with you that no one really knows—the night Meggan and I first met we ended up making out. At dinner we connected very quickly. There was so much mutual appreciation in the air. On some level we both felt that we had known each other forever. Much like Gwendolen says to Jack in *The Importance of Being Earnest*, we were overwhelmed by positive affection for one another even leading up to meeting. And, because we had connected on a heart level, making out seemed like a normal response. The next time we saw one another, and every time since, we have just been close platonic friends; we recognize that ours is not a romantic connection, but a deep and valuable friendship.

There are times when people come into our lives for one reason or another, and they are just the right person for us on an energetic or emotional level. It can be a connection over shared interests, or because you've moved somewhere new and are open to developing relationships, or because you are going through the same thing together. As Meggan discusses later, a strong connection with someone does not presuppose a sexual or romantic relationship. These are people you can love with all your heart in an open but platonic manner.

For example, I didn't consider myself close with Miranda, my friend Alex's girlfriend. We didn't have a lot in common, but she seemed to make him very happy so I embraced her in a kind but somewhat distant way. We would chat at parties; that was about it. Then, on July 13, 2012, Alex died unexpectedly of heart failure. I was devastated. My first call was to my recent ex-girlfriend, who was also close with Alex. The second was to Miranda.

I don't know why, but I knew I needed to connect with her above everyone else. We immediately bonded in a fresh way over our shared grief. We made travel arrangements together and went through the horrible ordeal of the next several days, including the funeral, several memorial events, and time with his family. All the while crying on one another's shoulders. We were inseparable for weeks, feeling like the other person was the most in sync with what we were going through. When I left NYC to work on the Obama campaign in Alex's memory, Miranda was quick to join me, and we worked in tandem on that effort as well. Weeks turned to months of us relying on one another in an intense and loving way.

We grew to the level of familiarity that married couples aspire to. We each knew what the other would want to eat on a given morning. If the other person stepped away for a bit, we implicitly knew whether they were crying or smoking (or both). Next steps for complex projects at work could be delegated to each other with a look or a nod. And when we needed to vent, the other person offered unconditional space and support. Not unlike what Meggan describes later in this chapter, our relationship became so deep so quickly because we both felt truly seen, known, and loved.

After months on the campaign we returned to NYC and continued to be close friends. However, as our grief morphed in different ways, so did our relationship. As His Holiness the Karmapa wrote, "Love evolves as circumstances evolve. Because times change, love changes, too."[1] We were no longer side by side at all times. We got to the point where we would see each other only once a month or so.

Miranda recently moved to New Orleans, so now we don't even see each other in person that often. When we do we can talk for hours, and it's clear our friendship was forged by more than shared loss. We still talk about Alex, his family, and other aspects of the horrible situation that brought us together, but there is more to our dynamic than that. Our relationship began through shared grief, but our love and friendship changed over time to accommodate our shared experiences.

On a lighter note, another example of this platonic love in my life is Uncle Gary. Eight years ago I was in a Boston bar watching the World Cup with my longtime friend Oliver. A man approximately our age came up behind us and asked if we had a good recommendation for a local beer. We got to chatting about Harpoon IPA and his summer in Boston doing research. Because he was new in town and seemed nice enough we invited him to a party with us that night.

Within 48 hours that man, Gary, became a regular part of our friend group. We would be out at a Mexican restaurant and Gary would march in and smash his fist on the table, shouting, "Tequila for my men, water for my horses!" Because he had a fancy research job with a stipend he often dismissed our offering to pay for these shots with a flourish, saying, "It's on Uncle Gary."

Because we only had a summer together in Boston we tried to make the most of it, and many incredible adventures were had. While our friendship began because Oliver and I were feeling open to chatting with a stranger, there was something about Gary that made him immediately click with us. Gary returned to Santa Cruz after that magical summer, but we are still in touch. When he comes to NYC he reaches out and we revert to our old dynamic, which is delightful.

I never would have developed these friendships if I hadn't been open to seeing Meggan, Miranda, or Gary with fresh eyes. With Meggan, I was just off the train, speaking at my first writers festival, and happy to have a friend. With Miranda, my world fell apart and she was one of the few people I knew who could join me in this uncharted emotional space. With Gary, I was just relaxed enough to let a stranger into my life, and I'm glad I did.

We often go through life lost in our own heads, plagued by the concern du jour. It might be the project at work we have to finish, or relationship troubles, or just thinking through our schedule, but more frequently than not we don't relax and appreciate the potential for love around us.

Meditation often gets a good rep for making people relax. I think that's valid, but it takes some time for us to feel that sense of peace in our "peaceful-abiding" meditation. The more you apply yourself to that experience, the more you can learn to relax with your strong emotions, fantasies, and discursive thinking on the meditation cushion. You realize that no matter what comes up during your meditation practice, you can relax. That level of relaxation naturally seeps into the rest of your life. When you are able to pull yourself out of being lost in your own head, you are more available to the world around you.

Through meditation you are creating a spacious internal environment that is awake and attentive, so you can appreciate your external one. Sakyong Mipham Rinpoche wrote, "True happiness is always available to us, but first we have to create the environment for it to flourish."[2] That is what we are doing when we meditate. We are creating the conditions for us to connect with ourselves and our world in a way that makes us truly happy. When we are able to relax in this way, appreciating and tuning in to our environment, we are discovering our basic goodness.

The view of basic goodness I introduced earlier in the book has a few aspects to it. The first, which we've already discussed, is that you are basically good. You're basically lovable. The second part is that you're not alone. Everyone else possesses basic goodness, including the neighbor that you love and your jerk of a boss and your ex-girlfriend. Every single person out there is just as much basically good as you are.

Not unlike you, they get confused at times. They don't always act from a place of goodness. They lash out, just like you do, and do things that harm themselves and others. It's sad that this happens, but from a Buddhist point of view the reason we do that is because we can't relax enough to be open to this inherent state. There are other ways to relax than meditation, but I have to give the practice credit: it does help you realize when you're acting out of confusion and causing a lot of harm. The self-awareness that comes with meditating can't be understated. But as you discover your neurosis you're also discovering that you're innately good.

If you're basically good and lovable and everyone else is basically good and lovable, that means that the potential to open your heart to the world is boundless. There will likely be many Uncle Garys tapping your shoulder at a number of bars asking for a drink recommendation. It's up to us as to whether we want to lean into our world and engage them. The question is, how much can you open your heart to love others, in a nonromantic way?

One way to experiment is by engaging someone new in conversation. This could be your neighbor down the hall who you keep running into in the elevator. Or the employee who just joined your company. Or the barista at your local coffeehouse. If that person rebuffs your attempt to chat, try someone else. But have a real conversation with them. Notice when you try to regulate what you're telling them or try to sound more glamorous than you actually are. Just relax and be yourself with this person over the course of five or more minutes.

This is an experiment in loving openly. You may find that this person is a creep and you never want to see them again. Or you may find out that your neighbor is wonderful and want to invite them over for a glass of wine sometime. See if you can remain open enough that a new platonic relationship can arise.

The more we can love openly, the more our friendships blossom. We don't often expect the same things from our friends as we do our romantic partners. We let our love flow freely, and not surprisingly, when we do, we find that it's often reciprocated in kind. Thus, when we go through a big breakup or a personal tragedy, it is these platonic loves of our lives that are there as rocks for us to lean on.

To some extent, I've relied on those friendships more than I have on my own family. That period of tragedy when Alex died mirrored when my father died. It was all a blur, but in both instances my friends were in and out of my apartment and life like nobody's business. They were there with whatever I needed—food, a hug, anything. I have no idea where I would be without the great platonic loves of my life.

The more we can love others in a platonic way, the more we are able to love people in a romantic fashion. Think about it: How quickly do you forgive your best friend when they don't text you back the same day? It's probably not much of an issue. You love them so much, and are so confident in your relationship, that you can relax and enjoy that dynamic whether they get back to you or not. Whereas if your new paramour doesn't reply to you in a few hours, you start sweating. You assume something is going wrong—they are becoming distant and will likely dump you soon. The difference here is attachment. You love your friends in an open, fluid way, where you may love your romantic partner in a more constrained, attached manner.

To return to the Sakyong quote, it is up to you what sort of environment you want to create for yourself, internally and externally. True happiness is always available, but not if you are continuously lost in your own head with that concern du jour. Meditation and other self-awareness practices help you tune in to the present moment, so you can appreciate your world as it is, and be available for these great loves of your life to enter. Through meditation we can create a very spacious internal environment.

The more self-aware you are, the more discerning you will be about your external environment as well.

You learn which friendships you want to cultivate, because those are the friends who are there for you through thick and thin, who understand you and see you for who you are, and yearn to support your journey no matter what it looks like. You may also learn which friends you might want to cut out or see less of, based on the fact that they do not prioritize your friendship in any way, or bring about negative qualities in you. If you feel uplifted spending time with certain friends, that is a good sign you should cultivate those relationships. If you feel drained at the end of an evening with them, you may want to examine those relationships more deeply. In this way, you develop an environment of support and love that can bolster you even at the toughest of times.

Ladyloves and Sacred Man-Friends

MEGGAN

Lodro! We did not make out! We kissed. Yes, we kissed the day we met. (And it was a warm, sweet, great kiss.) But that was how the evening ended; what matters even more is how it began. I was at dinner, ecstatic to be sitting next to Elisabeth Lesser, author of *Broken Open*, and Gail Straub at a restaurant in Woodstock. We were talking about Lodro, whom I had never met, and the interview we were going to do the following day. Suddenly, Lodro whisked into the seat opposite me and time seemed to stand still.

Now, let me pause for a moment to admit two things: first, I love sci-fi, and second, I don't believe in time. I admit this only because when I first met Lodro, for a split second everything else ceased to exist. It was like entering a time warp where I was entirely in the present (in slo-mo) but also somehow aware of a time long ago when I knew Lodro. There are some people we meet in life that don't feel "new" to us. They feel like people we recognize. People we are not meeting so much as reuniting with. That's what meeting Lodro felt like. It was as if we had found each other again.

When the initial connection is that strong, some feel that the concept of karma best explains how someone we have only just met feels like someone we've always known. *Karma* is a Sanskrit word that means action, work, or deed. It is closely associated with the concept of rebirth (past lives) and the concept of causality, which presupposes that our actions in the present moment affect our future. Simply put, the good we do in the present affects the potential of us experiencing good in the future. It's a cosmic form of checks and balances where actions with bad intent cause or create future misfortune, whereas actions with good intentions in the present allow that good to flow back to us. And what's more, as Paulo Coelho explains in his nearly autobiographical novel *Aleph*, "It's what you do in the present that will redeem the past and thereby change the future."

Since time does not really exist on a soul level, when we heal something in the present moment it simultaneously reaches back to heal the past. For example, in *Aleph*, Paulo Coelho's main character, also named Paulo, was a priest in a past life who sanctioned the murders of four young women under the pretenses of witchcraft. In Paulo's present life, hundreds of years later, he is destined to meet with each of the women he murdered in his past life and seek forgiveness for his actions now. This is the only way his soul can, in a sense, move forward, evolve, and be free. Or as Paulo explains,

"No one ever loses anyone." We all just keep meeting those unique souls who can instigate growth in our lives and evolve the soul.

As intriguing as it might seem, I am incapable of focusing on past lives. This one precious and unrepeatable life is captivating enough. I personally don't need to know the backstory, so to speak, when I meet someone I feel like I've known for far longer than either of us have been alive. But I do like to stay aware throughout the relationship of all the opportunities for me to grow. A strong, immediate, and powerful connection with someone does not presuppose a sexual relationship. Yet obviously, it makes one more likely. And sometimes we have to fumble through the physical to see if it's a part of why we have been led to meet someone (again). In my experience, a platonic or nonsexual relationship can be just as powerful and transformational as a sexual one. And for that reason, I have many soul mates in my life—both ladyloves and sacred man-friends whose presence is no less primary or foundational than my lovers or my eventual life partner.

In Plato's *Symposium*, the priestess Diotima teaches Socrates the philosophy of love. For Diotima, the highest purpose of love for another person is to help direct our mind to love for the divine. (Oh great, now Steve Winwood's "Higher Love" is blaring in my head.) Love, she explains, is the child of resource and need. It is the most useful tool we have to learn how to ascend from base thoughts to the more spiritual thoughts that occupy the heart. And this is what we need to do; it's what we are here for. Each person we encounter has a divine purpose to elevate our thoughts from attachments to external beauty to the eternal and more internal beauty of the soul. Her ideas of love are the origin of the concept of *platonic love.*

The Angel Medium had me at his tattoos. I was speaking in London at an event with many U.K. authors I had never met. The Angel Medium gave a spine-tingling, soul-stirring talk. I felt this immediate affinity. He mesmerized me. Later, the event director said the Angel Medium had heard me speak and wanted to have dinner with me. I felt giddy; ridiculous-schoolgirl giddy. The first thing he did when I sat down next to him at the restaurant was roll up his sleeves. (He was in Vivienne Westwood tartan!) There on each of his forearms were the two spiritual loves of my life, the Hindu goddess Kali and Saint Mary Magdalene. I knew in that instant that the Angel Medium and I were soul-family. I started planning our retirement.

Our relationship began where most friendships get to after years of knowing each other. The trust, the love, the intimate awareness of who we really are—it was all just there. What some friends have to earn or work toward, we were just gifted with. Since he lives in Scotland, we Skype, Facebook message, and Viber each other. The distance doesn't separate us in the least. We support each other with the spiritual gifts we each have. We promote each other whenever possible with the ardent and authentic love we have for each other's work. We believe in each other. We also swap pictures of our dream homes, potential outfits, and crazy powerful spiritual images—like the vesica piscis on the sacred well at Glastonbury. He and I are beloved to each other. And our relationship is no less significant just because we'll never actually marry or procreate. The significance comes from truly feeling seen. Known. Loved.

The most recent voice memos I received from the High Priestess of Desire were titled "Seismic Feminine" and "Grace Period." I could sense what listening to them would do to me. So I set aside a night when I could give what she had to share my absolute full attention. And I was so grateful I did. Because when the second memo ended, I cried (what my son calls "the happy cry"). I had never felt so held, witnessed, blessed. In our voice memos back and forth to each other, we get completely honest with where we are on all possible levels (since they're all connected): the physical, the emotional, the spiritual, the personal, the professional.

Her messages make me laugh—those laughs that come from the gut, the ones that clear the lungs and make me cough. And her messages move me to tears from the authenticity of our mutual effort to embody love more, no matter what. I did the happy cry after her most recent missives because I was flooded with an abundance that felt divine. Having a friend like the High Priestess of Desire provides a sense of wealth that leaves me in awe. My voice memos in response were titled "Divine Compensation" and "The Lucky Ones."

And just like the Angel Medium, the fact that we have a country between us doesn't minimize our closeness. We see each other several times a year, and in the meantime, whenever we catch up we might as well be next-door neighbors. It's a rare friendship that is entirely about expanding my soul. Given I'm a quintuple Scorpio (which, for those of you who don't speak astrology, basically means I'm all water—emotions, feelings, intuition, and intensity), many people feel overwhelmed by me. And at one point in my life this upset me. It inspired me to try to tone things down, to rein in the raw emotions. This of course was an epically futile effort. Trying to tone down who I am was like trying to siphon the ocean through a coffee stirrer. Yet once I fully accepted my own intensity, that's when I started meeting soul mates like the Angel Medium and the High Priestess of Desire. They exist as intensely as I do. We're emitting the same frequency. And my life is so much more for having met them (again). What finding soul mates like Lodro, the Angel Medium, and the High Priestess of Desire reminds me is that a foundation of love is necessary in order for me to love. It's the environment for happiness that Lodro writes about. So often, we focus an inordinate amount of time and attention on finding "the one." We have immense expectations of this "one": to be a tantric lover, a best friend, a mind reader, a soul pleaser, a sous chef, and a breadwinner. We're anticipating a village worth of goods and services to come from this one human soul. It makes me sweat just writing that all down.

We expect so much out of our life partners. But those expectations are at odds with the way we might really want to be able to meet them, to see them, to love them without demands, and to accept them as they are. I think to love our husbands, wives, partners, lovers, significant others in the way that truly inspires us, we have to begin to put equal weight in the worth of all the sources of love in our lives. Soul mate is not just the one we partner with for this lifetime, or try to. Soul mate is all of those loves, platonic or otherwise, that come (again) into our lives to teach us about why we're here. That remind us of who we really are and that give us the opportunity to expand our capacity to love, to grow as a soul.

In the Gospel of Mary Magdalene, Peter, one of Jesus' disciples, says to Mary, "Sister, we know that the Savior loved you more than all other women. Tell us the words of the Savior that you remember . . ." And Mary responds, "I will teach you about what is hidden from you."[3] This response from Mary has always echoed in my mind as the voice of love, as the action that love takes in our lives. Ultimately, we recognize a true love in our lives, romantic or otherwise, because it illuminates aspects of ourselves that we couldn't see on our own. The French mystic and theologian Simone Weil believed that "true friendship is a miracle." Throughout her adult life, she wrote letters to her friend Father Perrin, a Catholic priest who saw the genius in her theological work. Like Diotima's, Weil's philosophy on human love is that it has the potential to direct our minds and our hearts to the divine. For me, true friendship means being able to be real with each other—to be the raw truth (both the light and the dark) in the presence of another without the fear or shame of being judged. It means having the opportunity to see more of who we are—to both accept and be able to transform into more of who we are meant to become.

Instead of letters like Simone Weil's, I wrote e-mails. And he wasn't a priest like Father Perrin, but I did confess everything to him. He's the man who read my first book, *Reveal,* in the form of passionate e-mails for almost a decade before it was published. Our relationship began in a book, actually. I read his short story in an anthology we both contributed to called *Blue Jean Buddha* while I was on a pilgrimage to the Black Madonna and Mary Magdalene in France. I reached out to him in NYC once I had returned to San Francisco in an e-mail titled "The Handless Maiden." I needed to integrate the spiritual experiences I had on the pilgrimage. I needed a *copain,* a witness. I needed help believing that my voice might matter. The friendship Paul offered me in every potent and meaningful missive he wrote back was nothing short of a miracle. Our friendship saved my life. Not from physical death, but from that death so many of us endure caused by fear—the fear that keeps us small, and constricted to a cagelike amount of how much we can express of who we really are. I knew Paul's love was true because it freed me.

Over a decade later, I asked Paul to say a few words at my first book launch party in NYC. I can still feel the hush that came over the crowded room as he related our modern pen-pal love, and how salvific it was for both of us. I can still feel how riveted I was to his words, because the love they contained restored meaning to my life in a way that let me feel like the luckiest, most beloved woman in the room. The concept of becoming gold, of feeling truly wealthy, flooded my entire being. He is someone I am most grateful for in my life, and always will be.

During one of our recent dates, David and I visited the Cathedral of St. John the Divine on the Upper West Side of NYC. Some couples barhop, but David and I church-hop. St. John's was our second of the day. The moment we walked in we both stopped talking, struck by the visual impact of the gigantic artwork of the phoenix, made of metal and light, being installed into the cathedral. But then our amazement morphed into an even deeper awe when we saw the second phoenix right behind it. We asked someone nearby about the artwork, and we were told that it's a he-phoenix and a she-phoenix.

Something within underwent a massive renovation in the split second I realized that the phoenix didn't have to fly alone. I had always considered the phoenix to be a solitary bird. Its myth of bursting into flames only to be reborn from the ashes three days later has always resonated with me. From my years as an urban nun at seminary, and years alone on pilgrimage, I never considered the idea of being able to rebirth myself with someone else, who would burst into flames and reinvent themselves, body and soul, right beside me. For me these two massive phoenix lovebirds created more space for what's possible. And this is what true friendship does—it expands the myth of what we think is possible for our lives.

A conscious cultivation of the many ladyloves and sacred man-friends I have in my life allows me to have desires in a romantic relationship rather than demands. There's less expectation, more ease. I can be in right relation to a romantic love because I continue to give and receive from so many other sources. What I have always desired most is a love that can witness the truth of who I am. I know now, though, that love is the child of resource and need. It comes in so many forms, if we can be open to it, as Lodro expressed so beautifully. I know that I will never again narrow the space my soul inhabits by thinking there's just one soul mate out there. Every true friendship in my life is a miracle, a soul mate here to remind me of who I am and to give me the invaluable chance to love them, fiercely. Each true friendship creates a sacred container for our souls to reveal to each other what was hidden from us, what we couldn't see on our own. And to discover together, with compassion and trust, why we've been brought together (again).

Suggestions for cultivating your platonic loves

FROM LODRO

1. Buy them flowers or other gifts. Whenever I travel I make sure I pick up a few small gifts for friends, too, just to let them know they were on my mind while I was away.

2. Call them on holidays. I call each of my friends on Thanksgiving. I'm not entirely sure why I picked that particular holiday as sacred, but I'm guessing it has to do with me being grateful for their role in my life.

3. Always pick up the phone. To offer a safe space for your friends when they need to express themselves is a great kindness.

4. Nurture their loves. When someone I love has taken on a new romantic partner I always try to get to know him or her, independent of my friend.

5. Tell them you love them. Dropping the L word isn't that common between friends, particularly among straight men. But we usually don't regret the love we share with friends; we regret the words not spoken.

FROM MEGGAN

1. One of the greatest investments of my time is cultivating friendships. Invest as much time as you can either being with or communicating with your friends. This way you demonstrate the reverence you have for that person in your life.

2. Several of my ladyloves and I are pen pals. Send cards or letters filled with your gratitude and the love you have for your friends. (Though, as you know, I think voice memos work magic, too.)

3. Make lady dates with girlfriends with the same intention to show up the way

you would for a date with a potential lover. Dress up. Make it matter. And let it demonstrate to them how much they mean to you.

4. Try praying (or, if praying feels like a shoe that doesn't fit, try wishing) for your friends with a fervor you might have only used for your own life until now. Wish for every possible good to come your friends' way. By acting on my love for my friends by praying for them with all my heart, I began to receive my own answered prayers.

CHAPTER 7

How to Love Sacred Sex

This is the point where love becomes possible. We see the other with the eye of the heart, an eye not clouded by fear manifesting as need, jealousy, possessiveness, or manipulation. With the unclouded eye of the heart, we can see the other as other. We can rejoice in the other, challenge the other, and embrace the other without losing our own center or taking anything away from the other. We are always other to each other—soul meeting soul, the body awakened with joy.

—Marion Woodman and Elinor Dickson,
Dancing in the Flames

The Magic of Becoming One

Meggan

I didn't know what was happening. An indeterminate place deep within me was melting, or catching fire, and it illuminated this newfound territory inside me. It was a muggy summer night and I was on the couch with our foreign exchange student, Magnus. We'd felt an immediate connection when he had arrived the previous fall. That night, he rented a French movie we were both pretending to watch. Soon after I sat down beside him, he picked up my hand and gently kissed my knuckles, drawing each one slowly and deliberately into his mouth. The intensity of his concentration, his presence, commanded me to be fully present to his touch and to every sensation he created. That's when the melting started, and that's when I realized that my body was a far more mysterious landscape than I had ever imagined.

Magnus was my first love. And because I was a teenager, no fact or circumstance could possibly keep us apart; not even that he was Swedish and had to return home at the end of the summer. I went all Romeo and Juliet over the situation, pledging to anyone who said otherwise that our love would win. It wasn't just the "melting" that made him immensely special to me. We'd had another experience a month before, when we were visiting my older sister at her college, that first taught me just how much is possible when love fuels desire.

I couldn't sleep. My sister was snoring and had left me only a sliver at the edge of the bed. But mostly, my sleeplessness had to do with Magnus's proximity. He was on the couch in the living room. I wanted to be near him. I gave up trying to sleep and instead decided to use my imagination to do what I really wanted, which was to tiptoe out into the living room and kiss Magnus on his big forehead.

So I rolled over on my back, took a deep breath, and started to imagine every detail of walking out to him: I felt the cold wood floor on my bare feet and heard the creak of the floorboards as I approached my sister's bedroom door. I felt the hard metal of the old antique doorknob and the shift in the air as I carefully eased the door open. I imagined every detail in the living room, the paintings on the wall, the way the shadows fell across the furniture, and even the slight smell of mold in the old house. I saw and felt it all as I approached him. And then I knelt beside the couch, and softly kissed the center of his forehead as he slept.

The next morning, as we were folding a blanket in the living room, Magnus asked me if I had kissed him good night. I dropped my end of the blanket.

"I wasn't sure if it was real or a dream," he said.

"Where did I kiss you?" I asked, stunned and slightly freaked out.

"On the forehead," Magnus replied.

My mouth dropped open. I felt so much awe I had to sit down. I told Magnus then that I had only imagined kissing him good night—that I had never left my sister's room. "It was only in my mind," I told him. Neither of us knew what to make of it. But this strange kiss is what made me feel as though something sacred was between us. How could he have perceived something physically that had only happened in my mind?

Sex so often and for so many is purely a matter of anatomy. This part fits into that part, and the rest fulfills itself. My memories of sex education class from high school consist mostly of full-size diagrams of the male and female body—as if sex can be explained by just identifying the organs involved. I felt a mix of intrigue and inadequacy as I stared at the female body depicted in the diagram with key words written over key parts, revealing a language I didn't speak yet: *mons pubis, clitoral hood, vulval vestibule.*

I had ambivalent feelings about being in a female body. Until Magnus, I had never really experienced sexual pleasure. Like far too many, I had been sexually abused as a little girl, so my ability to dissociate was practically a superpower by the time I was in my late teens. Any physical encounters with boys up until the night Magnus kissed my knuckles involved me leaving my body to such an extent that I could barely feel anything—not a kiss, not a caress, not even sex.

So in sex education class as I scanned the diagram with all those Latin and foreign-feeling names for parts of the female body, I knew that for me sex would always be far less literal. And I knew I could only really experience sex once I was willing to actually stay present. The first and most primal relationship I needed to work on for sex to be good, much less sacred, was not with my sexual partner. It was with my own body.

As a theologian, and a spiritual mentor to women, I am acutely aware of the ways that religious ideas of the body have made for some seriously bad sex. All too often, exposure to more traditional religious paths creates a separation of the body and the soul. The body is perceived as less sacred than the soul. So, for example, there's a sense that asceticism (denying the body physical pleasures) is somehow more holy than listening to what the body desires. This idea then creates a sense of guilt if we do "indulge" in the bliss the body can provide.

One of the themes we discuss in REDLADIES is the sacredness of our bodies. The conversation invariably arrives at this very personal question we each have to ask ourselves: What does it mean for me to feel sexually empowered? For some, it means being able to have sex when it feels right and safe, whether it's in a committed relationship or not. Just being able to follow the instincts of a healthy libido without guilt or shame is both liberating and powerful. For other women, it's immensely important to only experience physical intimacy with committed partners. It doesn't feel like a loss or "sacrifice"; it's a way of expressing both their love for their own bodies and also their love for their partners.

Monogamy to them doesn't feel confining, but rather like a container that allows their relationship to thrive.

In either case what is most important is that they stay connected to what their body is communicating, because the body never lies. It has always intrigued me that so many ladies experience physical symptoms when their relationship is off or in some way dishonest. They might be able to convince their partner with words that "everything is okay," or that "their needs are being met." But inevitably, if that's not actually true, the body begins to communicate the dis-ease between them. And healing means getting clear about what they're feeling; it means telling the truth about what is really in their heart.

The most significant realization I have had that allows me to be present and embodied is the understanding that the body is not separate from the soul. Until death, the two are indivisible. The 19th-century mystical poet and printmaker William Blake wrote in his spiritual masterpiece *The Marriage of Heaven and Hell* that "Man has no body distinct from his Soul; for that call'd Body is a portion of Soul discern'd by the five Senses, the chief inlets of Soul in this age."[1] For me, an ultimate spiritual goal has been to become undivided, body and soul.

The metaphysical text *A Course in Miracles* relates that "the holiest of all the spots on earth is where an ancient hatred has become a present love."[2] This has been my experience in our modern world: we have been enduring an ancient hatred of the body. Whether that hatred originates from religious ideas or popular culture's unrealistic standards, the majority of people I have encountered on my spiritual path, both male and female, have had to work at learning to love their bodies again or for the first time. Whether they have experienced a form of abuse or not, they have had to find their way back to trusting their bodies. The wisdom of the body feels lost to them. It once felt lost to me. The bridge for me to return to my body, to transform "an ancient hatred" into "the holiest of all the spots on earth," was found in my heart.

In Dr. Karen King's translation of the Gospel of Mary, Mary Magdalene recounts to the disciples a vision she had of Jesus. In the vision, Jesus starts by praising her: "How wonderful you are for not wavering at seeing me! For where the mind is, there is the treasure." Then she asks Jesus how she is able to perceive him: "So now, Lord, does a person who sees a vision see it with the soul or with the spirit?" And Jesus answers, "A person does not see with the soul or with the spirit. Rather the mind, which exists between the two, sees the vision and that is what . . ."[3] (The next three pages of the Gospel of Mary are missing.)[4]

In my years at seminary, I was slightly obsessed with this excerpt of Mary's Gospel. I wanted to understand what Jesus meant by suggesting that "the mind" is where the "treasure" is, and what exactly "the mind" is that exists between the soul and the spirit, especially since he claims that this "mind" is what allowed Mary Magdalene to perceive him in the vision.

According to Jean-Yves Leloup's translation of Mary's Gospel, when Jesus answers Mary's question about how she sees him in a vision, instead of using the word *mind*, Leloup uses the word *nous*.[5] The Greek word for mind or intellect, *nous*, was far more complex than our modern understanding of "mind." The ancients didn't simply use the word to refer to our thoughts or brain functioning. The nous was considered to be the highest of all our faculties. Plato describes the nous as "that which is best in the soul," or "the soul's pilot."[6] The nous is that aspect of the soul that connects the divine to the human. It's the point of intersection between two worlds, or "the point of contact between god and man in the ground of the soul."[7] So the nous, then, is a spiritual sense; it is "the spiritual eye of the heart."[8]

Returning to Mary's Gospel using this concept of the nous, or mind, it would seem that the heart is the treasure. Not the heart as in the physical organ, but the heart as in the mystical awareness of love within us. The Christian mystic Macarius of Egypt, a 3rd-century monk and hermit, relates the primacy of the heart: "If the heart is at the center of man's being, then it is through the heart that man enters into relationship with everything that exists."[9] And Theophan the Recluse, a 19th-century saint in the Russian Orthodox Church, describes the function of the heart as the capacity to feel "everything that touches our being."[10]

I never ask my REDLADIES to do anything that I haven't first asked of myself. So that same weekend last winter when I met David, I asked the women participating in my REVEAL retreat to do a soul-voice meditation after we discussed the sacredness of the body. We went within and asked, *How can I become more embodied?* We all descended into our hearts and listened for the answer. I heard, so loudly, that there was a part of me that ardently believed I could only have a healthy balanced sex life with a partner. And I became aware of what I had forgotten—that sexual energy exists and thrives within me whether I'm having sex or not. Sex isn't ultimately an act; it's energy.

When I shared what had been revealed to me in the meditation, one of the ladies in the circle suggested I listen to Tom Kenyon's meditations on the Alchemies of Horus. She even sent me a copy after the retreat. I started doing the Alchemies of Horus (also known as Sex Magic) every night before bed. And still do. Through breath work and awareness, the meditation involves imagining a black snake and a gold snake crisscrossing back and forth between the chakras as they work themselves up from the base of the spine to the center of the brain. In a sense, this visualization moves the sexual energy at the base of the spine, also referred to as Kundalini, upward to the mind. It's a meditation that puts into practice the alchemical dictum "As above, so below."

This meditation is an effort to bring together what has been conceptualized as opposites: dark and light, body and soul, masculine and feminine. The result of using this meditation, of consciously working with my sexual energy instead of ignoring or denying it, has increased my vitality and health, and maybe most importantly, it has given me a profound sense of feeling sexually empowered. It's a power that's innate to being human, and once possessed, or reclaimed, generates immense healing.

For me, what makes sex sacred is the relationship I have to my own body. I practice the truth that my body has wisdom that is beyond language. It's a wisdom that knows itself completely. The body never lies. And the body is not distinct from the soul. The two are one in this lifetime. I try to stay in my body not just during sex but also in every moment.

Every breath is a spiritual practice. The entry point is the heart. The heart is that mediator between the realms of the ethereal and the material. The vision or eye of the heart is the essence of the soul, the nous. The more we are able to stay present in the body, in the center of the heart, the more we allow ourselves to truly connect to our partner.

Sacred sex in my experience is not about what Kama Sutra–like postures you employ, or what high-grade incense you've got burning. Sacred sex relies on our capacity to be embodied. Intimacy is difficult for many of us. Getting naked with someone can be awkward at best. We love to experience pleasure, to remember the sacredness of the body. And yet, giving and receiving pleasure can conjure some of our greatest insecurities and inhibitions.

From my spiritual mentoring work with women I know that I'm not alone in feeling fear and anxiety in the midst of having sex. What's rare is being able to be present to it. What's rare is loving and respecting ourselves enough to interrupt sex in order to really get intimate. We might not have any clothes on, but the true art of getting naked only emerges when we dare to be real. When we dare to stop when fear overwhelms us—no matter what stage of sex we're in. Yes, even then. That's true intimacy, not our dexterity in bringing our partner to climax. Intimacy is in our willingness to be vulnerable and expose ourselves in ways that go far beyond taking our clothes off.

There is so much "magic" we are still in the process of reclaiming. Remembering that the body and soul are one repairs an ancient rift in our understanding of what it means to be human. We are here to be fully present to all that we can experience in the body—from the physical bliss to the metaphysical mystery. That strange kiss I gave Magnus as a teenager was just the beginning. When we fully realize the power of being present to a heart in love, we will begin to participate in a consciousness that unifies and heals. We will begin to live out the reality that the body is sacred, because the body is the soul's chance to be here.

Bow Ties and Giving of Yourself Fully

LODRO

> We should have the attitude that sex is basically
> sacred; the spiritual implication should be there.
>
> —Chögyam Trungpa Rinpoche, *Work, Sex, Money*

When my first book came out there was a photo of
me that people took to. Somehow it would magically appear at my speaking events. I never meant it to be *the*
photo of me, although I quickly became known by it.
There I was, attired as I often am, in a plain white
button-down shirt and a bow tie. Years later, people still
come to my talks and when I speak with them after they
say in a disappointed tone, "I thought you'd wear a bow
tie tonight," as if a regular tie is the big letdown of the
evening. I do love a good bow tie, but the truth is it's a
bit of work to wear one all the time.

The beauty of the bow tie is that it's never going to be
perfect. You can treat getting dressed as a sacred act, taking the space and care to tie your tie. The positioning may
be a bit off, or it may come unraveled at a certain point.
But you see, its beauty lies in its imperfection. In this way
the bow tie reminds me of sex, in all its messy, beautiful,
intimate glory. In fact, if you loosely swap out *bow tie* for
sex in this paragraph, it's basically the same thing. It's an
affair to go down the road of choosing to wear a bow tie,
but it really is quite lovely when you do it.

The same can be said for sex—it never looks "perfect"
from an objective point of view (more on that in a moment), but can be so wonderful when you engage in it.
In the same way we can treat getting dressed as a sacred
act, we can view our sexual activity as a time to make the
ordinary extraordinary, simply through infusing the act

with our presence. Things may get a bit off or wonky at times when doing it, but its seeming imperfection is part of its awesomeness. When done in a fully embodied, intentional, and consensual way, sex can not only allow us to connect more fully with love, but it invites the other person we are with to do the same.

The other night I had dinner with a friend, Sarah, who is the curator for a website called MakeLoveNotPorn .tv. This site accepts and displays sex videos from people all around the world, aiming to celebrate the "messyawesomehumaness that is the sex we have in our everyday lives." It is a stark departure from typical, structured, by-the-book heterosexual pornography, which in my mind is not appealing. Since it's not me in the videos doing it, I can't say for sure, but typical pornographic versions of sex don't strike me as sacred.

After catching up about one another's love lives and common friends, Sarah and I ended up talking about work. Her job, in part, is to watch other people's sex tapes and cultivate a network of real-sex porn stars. I wasn't surprised when she said what she had learned during her time as curator: "The sex you have in your everyday relationships is the hottest sex there is." Why is it so hot? Because it's real. And the more we can tune in to what is real, what is going on right now in this moment, the more we are able to appreciate what is sacred.

As Chögyam Trungpa Rinpoche points out in the quote that opens this section, sex should be considered a sacred act. Here, giving of yourself is caring enough to be present with what is going on. As Meggan said earlier in this chapter, the more we are able to be present, in the center of the heart, in our bodies, the more connection we develop with our partner. When we are just *there* with someone, particularly when naked and aiming to pleasure one another, we are offering our heart to them. In that moment, when we show up so fully, that is love in an extremely pure form.

One of the richest ways to express love toward someone is to make love to him or her. You may be in a long-term committed relationship or you may meet someone at a bar and fancy him or her enough to go home together that night. A friend of mine, a holistic sex and dating expert, summed up my opinion on the latter scenario when she said, "I have no problem with sluttiness, as long as it is ethical." In either case, if you want to have a fulfilling sex life that is true to who you are, it's important to look at your intentions around sex, how you create safe environments for the act, and how you can utilize this intimate time with another human being as a sacred opportunity.

My teacher, Sakyong Mipham Rinpoche, has noted that knowing our intention is key in all areas of our lives. If you are going to start a new job, it's important to know why you are going into that line of work. If you are going to drink a lot of alcohol, it's important to know why you're aiming to get drunk. And when you are going to be in a relationship with someone else, in particular a sexual relationship, then it's important to know why you're engaging with the other person in that way.

There are a million reasons one might end up sleeping with another human being. You might be in love and want to express that physically. You might be heartbroken and want to try to get over your ex by (as cliché as it sounds) getting under someone else. You might meet someone you connect with deeply and want to explore that more in bed right away because you think you may never see them again. I myself have been in all those situations and more, and know there can be more than one reason.

I have a rule that I don't place judgment on any-one's reason for having consensual sex, but I offer cau-tion: knowing why you're doing what you're doing will be key in determining whether your experience is rich or messy. As with all things, knowing why we want to engage in an activity helps us clarify how we approach it. For example, the sexual activity when I am in a lov-ing, committed relationship is a clear manifestation of the hot and beautiful tenderness that exists between us. My intention is clear in these cases—to love and be loved by that person.

To pick an example of a time when I was not so clear about my intention, many years ago when I was heartbroken and trying to get over an ex, I was using (read: abusing) my sexual power because I was not wholeheartedly trying to connect with another person. I was fooling myself into thinking I was completely into this particular new sexual partner, and while I was certainly attracted to her on many levels, part of my heart was closed down. I was unaware of my intention, which was, in part, to try to distance myself from the feelings of pain around my breakup, and as a result I ended up hurting this woman, as well as perpetuating my own feelings of hurt.

Perhaps you have had a similar experience, where you were unclear about your intention and ended up making a mistake and hurting yourself and/or another. I mean, sex aside, it's hard to be in a relationship with someone and always be on the same page; we all make mistakes, misreading a situation or saying something unkind, and end up causing pain. I offer my story not to share what a jerk I was (although I was, let's be clear), but because I learned from that mistake and never re-peated it again.

Mistakes are valuable for one's spiritual path. When you make a mistake you can view that as an opportunity; your intention may end up coming into sharp focus. You see your situation for what it is, and know that you made the wrong move. The next step is to vow never to make that sort of mistake again and, if you can, try to make things right.

Sacred sex begins and ends with intimacy. If you can preserve the intimacy between you and your partner, before, during, and after the actual act of intercourse, then you have created a sacred environment within which you both feel valued and honored.

Creating a sacred environment for sex to take place begins well before any physical contact. It starts with that act of surrender, allowing your heart to soften and accept the other person for who they are. This tenderness, which is connected to bodhicitta, can arise at any moment. You could be at a bar and meet someone who you truly empathize with, and connect over some whiskey and a sob story or two. It can be with your long-term partner, who you have just had the best night out with, and now you're sitting on your couch recapping the highlights and lowlights of the day. It can happen with a complete stranger, a friend, a co-worker, or your neighbor. The point is that you let the walls down around your heart, inviting this other person in.

When we soften our heart and seek to connect with another human being, we are creating a safe space within which they can do the same. This softening and creation of a safe container is the first step in taking the physical act of sex into the realm of the sacred. From a traditional Buddhist perspective, we can say this is the view or intention. You are adopting the view that what you want to do with this person should be a sacred act, as opposed to unconsciously stumbling into it.

The next aspect is the activity itself. At some point in your sob story your new acquaintance leans over and kisses you gently on the mouth. Or you lie out across your long-term partner and begin to softly kiss her neck. Once the two of you have embarked on a consensual experience, don't be surprised if the communication that you have shared to date only heightens the intimacy and joy of the physical touch.

I've used the word *consensual* a few times now, but I want to clarify what I mean here. Consensual is not the absence of the word *no*. It's about being in tune with the other person and recognizing when they encourage certain behaviors and shy away from others. Some people love to talk dirty, be spanked, or assert dominance. Others are the exact opposite. You don't need to constantly ask, *Is this good for you?* (no one wants that), but you can check in on occasion and, more importantly, be present enough to notice when something that you are trying is being encouraged.

In order to create a strong container for sacred sex, it's important for you to be expressive, too. Communicate from the heart and let your partner know what you like, don't like, or are completely weirded out by. As Chögyam Trungpa Rinpoche wrote, "Communication cannot always be carried out by a verbal or mental process alone; sometimes the communication has to be physical. This should not be purely a biological matter of releasing pressure sexually but should be a question of learning psychologically to open one's whole being to somebody else."[11] If you can surrender and open your whole being to your partner, as difficult as that may sound, communication will naturally flow.

In my experience, the most painful thing someone can do in bed is shut down and stop communicating. The walls around their heart go up, and most likely yours will respond in kind. If you can remain in the moment with your partner (and that means no fantasizing about someone else, no trying to take yourself out of the experience by naming all the players on the Red Sox) and actually sink deep into your own body, then you invite them to do the same, thus sharing equally in the experience.

In addition to creating a safe container for sex physically, there's another benefit of communicating effectively in bed: you allow room for any emotional experience to occur. It has been said in Buddhist texts that at the point of orgasm you can experience a moment of being truly awake. You can rest your mind in your innate nature, the awakened state, and just be. That is a profound experience, and much more likely to last if you have been present during the act itself.

Alternatively, you or your partner may have a great swell of emotions at that time. It's not uncommon that with your physical release something deep in your emotional lockbox has been opened up, leading to laughter or tears. No matter what, if you can remain present you maintain that safe and sacred environment.

Having gone into your situation with an openhearted view and remained present during the activity itself, you can reflect on the experience afterward. Do you feel uplifted or depressed postcoitus? If you just met the person that night, do you feel more connected to them or less? If you have been with your partner for quite some time, did that feel fresh or rote? Checking in with yourself after such a potent experience lays the groundwork for how you want to approach this person and this activity moving forward.

The Dalai Lama has said, "Our prime purpose in this life is to help others. And if you can't help them, at least don't hurt them." I think that advice is an excellent marker for engaging in sexual activity with others. No matter the background of how you met them or where the connection might be going, you can use this parameter to judge whether you should hop into bed with them. If you believe that the experience will be beneficial for you both, based on openhearted communication between the two of you, great. If you feel like you are causing harm to yourself or your partner, then back off. The short-term pleasure of sex is not worth it.

In all things we need to work from the foundation of self-care and self-love, and then expand out to include whomever we encounter romantically. Sex is an incredibly special thing, and you deserve to enjoy it with people you care about, based on intentions that make sense to you, in a consensual and reciprocal manner, so that you leave the experience knowing that you are both better off for it. If you can observe these basic principles, you will have a healthy and joyful sex life, treating the act as a chance to connect with the most sacred aspects of your being.

Suggestions for more sacred sex

FROM MEGGAN

1. Exercise transparency. Foremost, be honest with yourself. Ask yourself if this is really what you want. If you hear or feel a no, then honor that as much as you would a yes.

2. Take a moment to light a candle, say a blessing, or just nod quickly to your soul. Sex is never devoid of soul. Every physical experience has the potential of being spiritual, of teaching us something that can lead to more awareness and more wholeness.

3. Be present. In my experience, the sacredness of sex is directly proportional to how present I am able to be in my body while having it. If your thoughts are more captivating, then take that as a colossal sign that now is not the best time to be intimate.

4. Sexual energy is a power. It's sacred energy that courses through you whether you are having sex or not. Find what lights you up and cultivate your sexual energy to enhance your creativity or to manifest what you want most in your life.

FROM LODRO

1. Realize that there is no wrong way to have sex, assuming it is consensual and ethical. Try to refrain from judging yourself— either your physical body or your wants and desires—during sex.

2. When you feel yourself getting distracted and you are no longer present with your body, come back to the breath. The breath is always available to you, so it is a resource that can bring you back into your physical form.

3. Postcoital conversations can be a lot of fun. Going beyond the generality of "Wow, that was amazing" and into the detailed realm of "I really liked it when you . . ." can inspire the other person's confidence in the bedroom and allows them clarity on what you enjoy. Communicating openly lets your partner know just how sacred the act is for you.

4. Try wearing a bow tie. Not a clip-on. A real bow tie. The care one puts into the simple acts of life, like tying such a tie, translates into even the most intimate of affairs.

CHAPTER 8

How to Love with a Broken Heart

> Rather than letting our negativity get the better of us, we could acknowledge that right now we feel like a piece of shit and not be squeamish about taking a good look.
>
> —Pema Chödrön, *When Things Fall Apart*

Moving Beyond Story Line

LODRO

One of my favorite movies is *500 Days of Summer*. It's a beautiful, well-written movie that tracks the beginning, middle, and end of a relationship. It's about heartbreak, fate, and all of the expectations that come along with being romantically involved with another human being. Our poor, heartbroken hero-turned-screenplay-writer Scott Neustadter based the film on a true story, and he opens it with this disclaimer:

> *Any resemblance to people living or dead is purely coincidental. Especially you, Jenny Beckman. Bitch.*

I rewatched the movie the other night and then looked up this Jenny Beckman, the aloof heroine, only to find an article written by Scott about how closely the movie paralleled his life. The best part of the article? The only time he ever saw his Jenny after their breakup was over dinner. They caught up about miscellaneous affairs and at the end he offered her his script. Sometime later Scott received a letter from Jenny saying how much she loved it and identified with the male hero. Despite Scott writing an entire movie based on their relationship, she didn't recognize herself in it at all.

When we suffer a breakup, there is a lot of story line involved. We look for things we could have done differently, reasons why it should have worked, early-warning signs that things were going to go south, all of it. That is certainly the case with me. And so often, as is proven in Jenny's case, the way we remember the relationship is only one version of a much bigger story.

I have never written about my broken engagement. It's a very painful topic, but I've primarily refrained because I don't want to upset my ex. We'll call her Blaire, as early on in our relationship she would make me lie in bed with her and watch episodes of *Gossip Girl*. Blaire would read everything I wrote, and edited much of it, but enough time has passed that I think she may never know this version of our story exists.

Not unlike the hero in *500 Days of Summer*, I was a big believer in fate. I moved to NYC in September 2008. One night, three weeks in, I went with a small group of friends to a bar in Brooklyn I had never been to before (and wouldn't go to again for many years). During the half hour I was there, a beautiful but drunk woman walked in and within minutes walked right up to me and asked me if I came there often. I laughed. "Is that your pickup line?" I asked. "Yes. That's my pickup line. Do you?" We both were buzzed, and we kissed that night.

Flash forward past a few semiawkward exploratory parties we attended. Now we're dating. Then we're a couple. Next we're living together. Then we're living in different cities for a bit. And finally we're reunited and engaged. In retrospect, my timing in popping the question was not ideal. We were very happy together, but she was applying for master's programs across the United States. Before we had to contemplate a move together I wanted us to be engaged. I was seeking solid ground in groundless territory—a relationship. She came home from work one night to find flowers everywhere, candles lit, and me on one knee in a suit. We had an amazing home life and I wanted to propose in our shared apartment. As I went through my heartfelt, well-rehearsed speech, our dog came over with the ring around her collar. Blaire said yes, and we went back to that bar in Brooklyn to celebrate.

She decided to leave NYC for a fully funded one-year program in Chicago. She also decided that I shouldn't uproot my life in New York for those nine months; we planned to move back in together in the spring. I paint the happy picture above because that is how I remember our relationship; it was lovely and she encouraged me to be a good person. I am forever grateful for that. At the same time, I still carry a lot of confusion, pain, and anger around our breakup. Six months apart, after doing not too good a job at visiting each other regularly, I arrived in Chicago. We made love, watched television on her bed, and then she got an e-mail from her mother asking about when they might go to London over the summer.

That led to what (I believe) we both thought would be an innocent conversation about summer plans and when she might be able to move back to NYC. Things took a bad turn a few minutes later. The question must have been in her mind for a long while, but it was the first time I had heard it said out loud: "What if I don't want to come back to New York?"

I got defensive, while she felt cornered by my expectation that we would live there and not London or somewhere else. I continued to try to pin things down; she continued to desire freedom. I was trying to set dates for a potential move to a new NYC apartment; she was contemplating traveling the world. In other words, she wasn't ready to marry me, and we had somehow stumbled into the realization together, at the same moment. We took a long walk, and after an hour or two of continued escalation the simple vacation planning had snowballed into her breaking our engagement.

I'm not proud of what happened next. I rarely decide to use the word *devastated*, yet I think that's a lovely word to describe my mental state at this time. I got on the next flight to NYC, sat in the back, and began bawling. The flight attendant gave me a few bottles of scotch once she saw what a mess I was. I drunk-Skyped a few friends from the plane to tell them what had happened. I landed at JFK, got in a cab, and went on a drinking spree.

The next weeks were a bit of a blur. We weren't fully broken up; it was a momentous decision that came out of nowhere, so we gave ourselves a few months to see what would happen. The more time that passed, the more Blaire felt confident that not marrying me at that time made sense. I begged for a reason—what had I done? She had none; our relationship was good. I was just not the right person at the right time. After three and a half years together I was alone with a broken heart.

But I wasn't alone. I had good friends, and whiskey, and *Game of Thrones*, and the story lines. Oh! The story lines! I had ways of winning her back swimming through my mind. I had the pivotal moments that could have broken us up. I had a bad case of the "whys": Why did she feel like she needed to go to London without me? Why couldn't we patch this up? Why did she tell me that she wanted to spend the rest of her life with me if she didn't really mean it?

The reason I love the story of Scott Neustadter and Jenny Beckman so much is that Scott clearly solidified his story of how the relationship came to be, the good times and the bad, and exactly why it went south. Yet Jenny must have had a completely different version of the story if she couldn't even recognize herself in the script he wrote about their time together.

I am guessing Blaire has a very different version of our time together. Maybe I pulled away over months of being apart, becoming an arrogant traveling author and never making the time for her. Or maybe she changed so dramatically in her master's program that I was no longer the type of man she was interested in. Or maybe what I categorized as a loving, spacious, good relationship was not her version of it. Blaire has her story. And I have mine. And neither is unilaterally "right."

When you go through a breakup there is no definitive answer to the "whys." The cracks that enter any relationship, romantic or otherwise, come in a million different ways and add up. Sometimes one obvious reason for a breakup (*He cheated on me*) is based on a thousand unspoken reasons (*I wasn't there for him during his father's death; He started feeling like he couldn't talk to me anymore; I was open with him about wanting to be more intimate and he blew me off*).

Later on, Meggan will discuss how it's not the heart that breaks, but the ego. The ego is the part of you that looks for the big "why"—that reason that if you can just discover it, things will feel less confusing and painful.

The ego is what made you and your partner into a solid, untouchable "couple," as opposed to two people who are constantly changing and evolving, ideally alongside one another. The ego is what can cause us tremendous pain, if we feed it with constant story lines and fantasies about what we could have done differently. When you let go of the ego, with its myriad versions of "why," you are left with a feeling of vulnerability. You are left with tenderness. When we are with someone, we believe we will stay that way, that we will not know disappointment, and thus have provided our vulnerable heart with some protective armor. Then that person leaves and we feel like a wreck of a human being. A broken heart is really just our natural heart stripped of its comfortable relationship armor. It's not a good feeling, from a conventional point of view, but it is good for us.

The Buddhist teacher Pema Chödrön has said that this experience of a broken heart is similar to that of the raw and wonderful feeling of bodhicitta discussed earlier. This bodhicitta, or open/awake heart, is our natural state. We always have the chance to be open, even when we're in pain. Pema Chödrön wrote, "Sometimes this broken heart gives birth to anxiety and panic, sometimes to anger, resentment, and blame. But under the hardness of that armor there is the tenderness of genuine sadness . . . This continual ache of the heart is a blessing that when accepted fully can be shared with all."[1] When you allow yourself to feel this natural ache you understand how to see your own way through suffering, into that openness, that bodhicitta, which is liberating for yourself and also allows you to connect more fluidly with other people.

We all have our go-to thing we do when we feel that pain, in order to numb or distract ourselves. Maybe you're like me during my broken engagement period and turn to alcohol. Or maybe you try to boost your self-esteem by hooking up with other people. Or you hibernate in your apartment alone and binge-eat junk food, or binge-watch television. Or you do the opposite: you get on the next flight out of town. Whatever your specific method may be, it's worth looking at whether that is truly helpful.

In my experience, when you try to forget that special someone with a distraction like alcohol, you just wake up the next day hungover and in more pain because your body and mind feel woozy. You're not going to avoid the pain of a broken heart, so the best thing to do is sit there with it.

I realize that sitting with your pain is easier said than done. Years later, when I went through a similar breakup (and all the abandonment issues that were brought up from the broken engagement) I knew that the best way to see myself through to the other side of my broken heart was to take the time to rest.

I would notice the pain of missing that person, my partner, who was no longer someone I could share my life with, and the sinking feeling that occurred in my body. When that would happen I would lie down and breathe into it. I wouldn't entertain the story lines that came up. Quite the opposite—I would return to the sinking feeling. And then, as if I had said some magic spell, the sinking feeling would lift and I could go about my day once more. By diving into the heart of what I felt, I ended up feeling liberated.

Love Is Not Enough

MEGGAN

I remember the moment vividly. We were facing each other, and our Jungian therapist was sitting off to the side between us. My son was asleep in his stroller to my right, as usual. He was seven months old, and we had been in therapy since shortly after his birth. I was trying to recover from what the therapist had just mirrored back to me. It detonated like a bomb inside my heart. I had been aware of it for a while, but as timing goes, I couldn't really accept it until that moment. Here's what the therapist said: "You can't fight for a relationship when only one person is in the ring." She was looking right at me. I held her gaze as my heart continued to disintegrate. My love, my partner, my husband, my closest friend couldn't look at me. The truth was too heavy and hurt too much.

We were good people. We weren't always able to be good to each other, but we were never cruel. Even in our most raw and human moments, moments where we met with sides of ourselves we never knew existed, there was still a glimmer of that initial intention we had set for our relationship—to be a source of support in moving past our individual fears. We both were eager to evolve, to know ourselves more deeply. We had a lot of love for each other and we had a gorgeous baby boy whom we each had made our priority. There was so much beauty, so many signs, such huge blessings, and support from our families on both sides. This is why everyone wanted a reason, a dramatic and clear transgression, or some sort of fundamental betrayal that made our divorce, or "conscious uncoupling,"[2] inevitable. But clarity around why our marriage ended is something I'm only finding now, four years later.

It took months to acclimate to the truth: I was alone in my marriage. It took months of continuing to find a way to "save" or "fix" us, of sobbing in the shower with the door locked and praying with unprecedented ardor, for direction about what to do next. There was so much love—I couldn't understand why we weren't able to find a way to make our marriage work. Finally, the day came when my husband was able to tell me his truth. He loved me. But he couldn't sustain the sense that this marriage was right for him. The ambivalence had been tormenting both of us. He asked for us to separate. Several weeks later, I moved into a one-bedroom apartment with my then ten-month-old son and began one of the hardest transitions of my life.

The spiritual being in me wanted to bypass this part. I wanted to connect to the divine, to meditate, to go to that place within me of unfaltering, undiluted love about ten million times a day. I wanted to spiritualize the experience of grief, to make it this epic gift and opportunity, instantly. I wanted to take the pain, the raw, seething depths of it, and transform it into palaces of light and wisdom. I wanted to build a cathedral inside me and spend the rest of my life there on my knees. But this was not what my soul wanted for me. Every time I went within and asked—or more like pinned my soul against the wall—for clarity about how to move through this, I heard a definitive command: *Be where you are.*

I was in pain. And the only way through the pain was to feel it all. I couldn't let the pain diminish the good. I couldn't let the outcome of our relationship overshadow the real light we shared. I couldn't demonize him. I was conscious of the risk in saying "I do." My soul had said yes. I was not a victim. I couldn't skip the work and go straight to the diamond this pain would create, nor could I write off our relationship as just a colossal mistake. I knew that for me, healing could only happen by letting the pain come. I had to endure the flames.

Everything that was false fell away. Stifling my own needs to first meet others' was a well-trodden path I could no longer afford to take. I had to be willing to lose the affection and support of others. I had to get steel-like and brave. I had to remain intimate with that still, small voice inside me.

What I grieved losing most in our process of conscious uncoupling was being in a family. I would see a man with a child riding on his shoulders with his partner walking hand in hand beside him. Or I would see a family of four eating at a restaurant beside my son and me, at our little table for two, and just ache for the symmetry of their togetherness. My real kryptonite was holidays. No matter what the holiday, I inevitably fell prey to an awareness of feeling broken. And the question I so desperately wanted answered would start to haunt me again: Why was my love not enough?

For the past several Thanksgivings, I have been invited to join my brother-in-law's family in Connecticut while my son celebrated with his father's family on Long Island. I once suggested that we practice a tradition my mom always insisted on, that each person take turns sharing what we're grateful for. On a recent Thanksgiving, my little sister brought a large felt turkey hat from the parade in NYC. So for the gratitude tradition, I suggested that we each share while wearing the turkey hat. My little sister and her husband went first. They had been married the summer before. So, each expressed gratitude to have a partner in this life. They were both emotional in ways that was rare for them to display.

My brother-in-law's parents were sitting facing each other on either end of the dining room table. His father was the last to share, and he commanded our attention. He started with gratitude for his family, for both of his boys and the fact that they had found their life partners. He was grateful for his work—that he worked with people he had created meaningful relationships with over the years. He had been addressing all of us up until this point, moving his gaze around the table. But suddenly, his gaze had one focus.

He looked across the length of the table at his wife as if she were the only other person in the room. Everyone fell silent. He started to speak, and then stopped. His head bowed, as if the weight of what he needed to say was overwhelming. I thought about the fact that they had survived a separation—that just being together again was some sort of miracle. Then he looked straight at her, with tears in his eyes, and banged his fist on the table. "You," he said with a force that sent chills through me. "You are what I'm most grateful for," he declared, as the little white chef hats at the tip of each turkey leg started to tremble from all the emotion pouring through him.

Jungian psychoanalyst Murray Stein describes a marriage or long-term partnership as a relationship that provides the opportunity for transformation. He relates that for it to survive and grow in dynamic ways, it must contain a mutual image of integration and wholeness. It doesn't have to be an image of traditional family, or of a joint creative endeavor, but it's an image or a vision, Stein says, "that holds conscious and unconscious, masculine and feminine, good and bad, in a frame of joined polarities."[3] A relationship with a shared image of a life together serves as a container, like the alchemist's cauldron. The coming together of these two form a third, which is "a vital presence, the spirit of the union, the irrational foundation of the joint enterprise."[4]

My marriage had a lot of love, and love continued to build all throughout our conscious uncoupling, and grows still now. But what my marriage didn't have was an "irrational foundation" that allowed us both to believe in this love, to choose this love in order to be devoted to this one person for the rest of our lives. Love is not enough because that love needs a vision to live into. The ferocious temerity I witnessed in that fist slam to the dinner table—the fight to choose this one person again and again—wasn't just about love. What allowed them to survive a separation and the many daily fires that had made that separation necessary was a shared vision of a life together—a shared vision of what that love they have for each other is here to create and manifest. Family constellated their world. It was the "third" between them that they each had devoted their lives to, the something more that each would fight to protect. They share a commitment to this relationship and a belief in its power to transform their ordinary lives into something extraordinary that neither could have created on their own.

The legend of Mary Magdalene leads to a small seaside village in the south of France. Supposedly, after the Ascension, Mary Magdalene journeyed to Rome to testify before the court of Tiberius Caesar that Jesus had risen from the dead. After bearing witness to Jesus' resurrection, she continued her ministry throughout the Mediterranean. She eventually arrived in the Camargue region of France with Mary Jacobe, Mary Salome, and Sarah, "the Egyptian," in a small seaside town that is now named in reverence to them, Saintes-Maries-de-la-Mer.

The cross of Camargue (la Croix de Camargue) from that region in France is composed of a cross at the top, a heart in the middle, and an anchor at the bottom. The cross represents faith, the heart signifies love, and the anchor is a symbol of enduring hope. I wear this cross in memory of Mary Magdalene's ministry but also because it reminds me of the alchemical trinity that helps my soul root and grow in love. It reminds me that love is a divine gift and an answered prayer, but it alone is not enough when it comes to romantic love. Love needs to be inspired by a tangible, visible faith. It needs to be believed in. And love needs to be anchored to a hope that provides an "irrational foundation," a clear vision of becoming more because of this relationship and of being in greater service to the divine.

Recently, I was speaking at an event with Dr. Robert Holden. I sat in the front row during his keynote with my red pen at the ready. He commented about the fact that we often refer to a breakup or the end of a relationship as "heartbreak." We use the expression when we're hurt or disappointed in love: *My heart's broken.* It's an expression that mirrors the pain but that perhaps doesn't mirror reality. What he suggested is that it's not actually the heart that breaks; it's the ego. The heart is limitless and vast, capable of loving with depths we too often can't even fathom. But the ego has clear limits and can break or even shatter at the end of a relationship.

I felt aware then that those feelings of being broken that used to sometimes overwhelm me came from my ego. My ego was the one wearing shiny red shorts in the boxing ring and didn't want to give up the fight. My ego has written many story lines, as Lodro so powerfully related. But fortunately, my soul has a story, too—a vision. And from time to time it breaks through the ego's sense of loss and sees the invaluable gain. Take a moment a couple of years ago when my son's father was up late on Christmas Eve at my apartment, putting together the pieces of the toy kitchen we had bought our son. He had started to sweat—the pieces of stubborn wood weren't fitting into place. Then, right in the midst of his struggle, this deep and genuine love for him started to suffuse me. It hurt, in this exquisite way, to look at him. Because I could see—I mean, it really sunk in as I watched him— that he has suffered alongside me through all of this. He has had his own story lines. His "whys." Compassion and forgiveness flooded me. And then I felt this ache of expansion, this crazy-huge inheritance, as if wings were slowly breaking through the walls of my heart.

My capacity to love was greater because of our re-lationship. We may not have the relationship my ego had wanted, but my love expanded in that moment to include even this. To accept this as the diamond it has always been—pain and loss included. Love was not enough to save our marriage, but love remained. I could hear then my soul whispering its own story line. The truth that the love we cultivate in a relationship is ours. We get to take it with us. And there's no moment more abundant than when we have the strength to be held by the love that will never leave us; the love that surges up to meet us from within.

Suggestions for sitting with a broken heart and "conscious uncoupling" (aka saving the love, transforming the relationship)

FROM LODRO

1. Don't engage in the usual things you do to escape pain. Write down the behavior you're going to change: *Do not party too hard;* or, *Do not shut everyone out;* or, *I won't throw myself into work.* Post that short sentence somewhere you will see it every day.

2. Practice self-care. Get more sleep than you think you need. Your body is processing a lot of pain. You need to allow it time to rest.

3. Eat at least three meals a day. When I am grieving, either over a relationship, a death, or anything else, I have a tendency to not eat. I've learned that this only depletes, so now I make sure I have snacks on hand, so there's no excuse.

4. Meditate. I know I'm kicking a dead horse, but meditation allows you time to be with your own mind and heart, as it is, without judgment. It teaches you to be with what is, not what could be.

5. Exercise. You can go to a yoga class or for a short run around the park. Whatever gets you out of your habitual space and allows you to use your body. It also enables you to feel good about your body, which may be important if feelings of rejection come up.

6. Talk to friends. My friends know I am not seeking advice or plotting how to get back together with my significant other, but just need sympathy, which they provide in spades.

7. When you feel stuck, it might be worth looking in the mirror, placing your hand over your heart, and saying, "I will love again" three or seven times. There is power in proclaiming things out loud. Doing so serves as a reminder that you always have the ability to love, either romantically or in other ways.

8. When strong feelings arise, like despair or heartbreak, don't do anything. Just rest. Breathe normally. Let them wash over you like a wave. You will be able to see your way through them. I promise.

From Meggan

1. It was rarely easy, but the single most powerful and significant exercise I asked my son's father to do with me each week as we were "consciously uncoupling" was to spend one hour on Sunday evenings to talk. During each talk, we would address three categories: our personal development, our work as co-parents, and three gratitudes. We each shared for ten minutes on each of the three topics and always used "I" statements for where we are in personally moving through this transition of our relationship. This created such beauty and space for

forgiveness during some of the darkest and most difficult times in the evolution of our relationship.

2. Forgiveness, like grace, can't be contrived or faked. But we can help create the conditions for forgiveness to arise. For me, it meant going within daily to dig through the layers of my pain and really find the root. Forgiveness both for myself and for him finally came when I realized I didn't have to stop loving him. The conditions under which I can express it have merely changed.

3. Self-care is so crucial for moving through a divorce or breakup. I got very fierce with my time to take care of myself. I increased massages, going to the gym, and long walks. I also made sure to set up lots of what I call lady dates, where I meet a friend or two for dinner. I also leaned into activities I love: writing, reading sexy-vampire books, and traveling.

4. Surviving the holidays postdivorce or postbreakup is all about re-creating the traditions that mean the most to you. Find family or loved ones willing to participate in the tradition that really represents "home" or "family" to you. Reframing or redefining what family is or who family can be transformed my experience of the holidays. Family to me isn't just that intimate nucleus of parents and child. Family is whoever and wherever I feel at home.

CHAPTER 9

How to Stay in Love at All Times

Love is not love until it's unconditional.

—Marianne Williamson, *A Return to Love*

Becoming Beloved

Meggan

"Close your eyes," David said, while his remained fixed on the road. And because he was the one asking, I did. Oddly, it felt good to surrender control. I trusted him. And I liked getting the chance to demonstrate that. We were speeding along a winding road, so it was a little scary, but the fear gave me that thrill of feeling more alive. Soon, he slowed the car down and turned. Then he said, "You can open them now." The back roads we took all morning were not to avoid traffic as he had suggested. All along he was actually leading me to the National Shrine of Our Lady of Czestochowa, home of a Black Madonna.

Sometimes when I try to imagine what my heart must look like after all this clumsy human loving I've done, I conjure an image so misshapen and scarred it no longer has walls. And sometimes that leads to feeling like I'm irreparably broken. But as I went down on my knees beneath the Black Madonna's icon, my eyes closed and all I could see of my heart was a wide expanse, an endless field, and a space so vast that I couldn't grasp how much it actually contained. In that moment, the brokenness felt like a requirement. All that pain was the perfect devastation I needed to reach this bliss.

I've spent most of my life as a scholar and pilgrim to the divine feminine—both potentially isolating endeavors. I would bet scholars and pilgrims have very similar dating tendencies: next to never. I have tried and painfully failed many times to figure out how to be in relationship to that divine love I experience in sacred scripture and on pilgrimage, while also loving a human man at the same time. So having those two efforts finally align, having David lead me to the Black Madonna, having him on his knees right there beside me, I've never felt so undivided. I've never felt a peace as deep.

Getting to love someone is both a gift and an assignment. In a way, since we can't contrive who our heart claims as beloved, it's a calling and a divine purpose to love. And it's not always easy. When we love this much we want to know that this love will always be in our life. Yet for me, happiness within a committed relationship seems to require that I accept the separations and distances our lives will always ask for us to endure from those we love, whether it's death or just time apart. If I can accept the necessary separations, I can embrace this love all the more passionately. In a way, happiness in love is maintaining a paradoxical mix of full commitment and nonattachment. Letting go of what this is going to become and just being fully present to what this is right now seems to work like sacred alchemy for me.

Love—true love—means no longer waiting. This has been my soul's koan from the start. True love isn't about finding that magical (mythical) someone who will transport me and evaporate my problems like a miraculous healing balm. True love starts from within. True love is when I see all those judgments and barriers that have kept my heart barricaded for what they really are— opportunities for my love to reach where it never has before. Every broken and closed off aspect of us is just another chance to exercise our capacity to love. Practicing, with devotion, that ability for us to let love reach within us where it has never been is the inner work that transforms our experiences with the people we encounter.

So often when we allow someone to remain in our lives who belittles our potential, treats us unkindly, or really doesn't get who we are, it's a reflection of the need for our own love (within us and for ourselves) to expand. We can get disappointed; we can gnash our teeth and pull our hair because we are so distraught over the perceived lack of love this person is demonstrating. We can get very "Why me?" I know I have. But when I began to see that the people who disappointed me were actually giving me an opportunity to look at my own lack of self-love, my whole life and all my relationships drastically shifted.

When I edited the moniker of my status from single to indie mom, I acknowledged that I may not have any control in a partner's choice to remain in a relationship, in love, but I have complete sovereignty in choosing how I will respond. I can use my indie mom status to benefit again from the space I'm afforded by being single and not in a relationship. And I can practice the trust needed to not be afraid that I'll remain indie, as in, alone. I can practice a Disciplined Hope that everything is *kairos*; everything is divine timing. And I can choose to trust that what's next, and who's next, is only more love.

My adventures in dating, from the blind date with my dad's look-alike to my experiments with Tinder, reminded me of the importance of staying open. When the spirit of the quest in each date was simply to meet someone new, I had a good time. And I even sometimes got a taste of the kind of relationship I really desire. When I showed up expecting to meet (and interview) my next potential life partner, I tanked. Letting go of, as Lodro puts it, "the shark of fixed expectations" frees us to have new experiences.

As an indie mom, and divorcée, I got buckets of unsolicited advice about how to find love. Staying open meant trying out new ways to meet men. And also, it was essential for me to temper that openness with those quiet but infinitely loud whispers I could only hear from within, and ultimately trust my own guidance. On the surface was a fear that I would never meet someone I could love as much as I had loved. But deep within, beneath the drama of that idea, I believed that the best was yet to come. Deep down, I had this steel-like faith that I would meet someone not because I was in the right place at the right time, but because I was fully revealing who I am and doing my darnedest to love every inch of me, the light and the dark. I trusted that someday someone would be able to join me in that effort. And would let me love him with all that I am.

If finding a meaningful love is what you want, I think a powerful practice is to really get clear about how you want to *feel* when you're with that new person. And then as soon as you have clarity about how you want to feel, start doing all you can to allow yourself to feel that way already. Giving yourself what you hope and desire someone else will give you becomes the greatest tool for knowing you've met someone significant. Rather than a certain physical trait or financial standing, you'll be able to recognize a relationship worth investing in because this person adds to, covets, and maintains those precise feelings you've wanted most to experience.

Your self-love allows you to remain loyal to your own soul, to tend and let flourish an inner garden that will remain verdant whether this lover leaves or remains in your life. Self-love creates that delicious distance between you as partners—those weekends when you do things apart; those experiences you continue to have on your own—so that you can cross that distance together and get to know each other again and again. Self-love while falling in love allows you to remain stable (more often) and lets you never forget that you are your truest source of love, not the other person. This radiant soul that has come into your life is simply overflowing an already filled heart.

I think the sweet, secret trick to happiness in lasting relationships is to be willing to betray your partner's needs in order to never betray your own. Sacrifice and martyrdom just don't pan out. If you're sacrificing what you truly need in order to fulfill your partner's perceived needs, trust me—your partner isn't getting what they need either. Sure they might get what's needed in the moment, an ego boost, or support of some sort. But ultimately, fear is at play. You're afraid you'll lose your partner if you don't meet their needs, or they're afraid to do something alone or in new ways. And betraying yourself to meet their needs actually keeps your partner from growing.

Relationships, especially lasting ones, give us the immense opportunity to really choose how we are going to show up. Are we going to become addicted, and dependent on this love, and live out our deepest fears? Or are we going to allow this love to let us amplify our freedom?

Will we meet this love with the highest version of who we are, no matter what?

We so often get myopic about love. We focus on whether or not we have a partner and fail to see all the love already and always present. Not just the love we meet from within, but also the limitless love of our closest friends. They can remind us of what we want most for ourselves, especially when we're settling or compromising in a relationship. They help us remember what can be so easy to forget when we've been alone for a while: that we are worthy of love, that our low points and accomplishments are witnessed and shared, and that we will meet someone who can really appreciate the unicorn of who we are. The deep love I have for the women and men in my life that I am so fortunate to call friends serves as this invisible but no less real safety net that's always there. I can take more risks because of them; I can dare more greatly in love because they are there for me as I am for them.

As a lover of love, it has hurt to realize that love is not enough in a lasting romantic relationship. Love needs a vision, an image of unity to live into. Love is divine and also it needs our very human faith to stay alive, or even more, to be able to resurrect. We have to not only believe in the power that brought this person into our life, but also in the relationship's unique capacity to transform us for the better.

My favorite story from the New Testament is in the Gospel of John, chapter 20, titled in my version of the Bible as "The Risen Life."[1] It starts with Mary Magdalene alone, noticing that the tombstone had been removed. She may have been afraid. She was human, distraught and weeping at the loss of him. But nothing mattered more than finding her way to be with him. I have always loved that she was the first one to notice that his body was missing. She revered his humanity. She cared deeply to see his actual flesh, his bones. To her, all of him was beloved.

I have always loved that she could see the two angels who stood where his head and feet had been, like two pillars of light in the dark of the tomb. She was a woman who witnessed the human and the divine. Both. Equally. And I have always loved that she couldn't see him standing right there beside her until she heard her name in his voice. It was only once he recognized her, acknowledged her, and revealed himself fully and first to her, that she could see his eternal face. It's for this reason that the saint Mary Magdalene has always reminded me of love—redivivus love. We so often think our love has died. Sometimes, many of us give up. Shut down. But if we can let our faith and hope in love carry us through the night, we can see the truth again. Love never dies.

I'm writing this on her feast day, July 22. Her love story has always felt distilled in the word *beloved.* And the way she was there at the tomb, in the dark—this has always been an inner compass for me. That she was there when no one else was can be seen as a metaphor of the divine feminine, as an attribute that we all contain. Her effort of being there at his death, in the dark, alone, seems to implore me to let love reach where it never has before. And that there's no reason to wait—there's no excuse or judgment that can keep love from overwhelming it. Faith in love wins. And as Dr. Robert Holden relates, "Love reveals that you exist in love, always."[2] We often feel disconnected, alone—even in a relationship and more while we're single. But the truth is that love is always here for us, within us. We only need to anchor to the faith that such abundance could be our birthright.

We only need to believe that this is our fundamental nature. To forget and then remember, to lose and then to find, sometimes outside us but ultimately within us, that love that is love that is love.

Love, true love, means no longer waiting. This has been my soul's greatest mantra. Waiting suggests I am not worthy enough, or not good enough yet to be loved. Waiting suggests that someone outside of me has to do the work for me—has to just appear and shower me with magical light rays of love. When in truth, that love I have always longed for is my own. It's the love that I can only give myself. So don't wait to prove anything to yourself or anyone else. True love is what you can choose to give yourself right now. Not perfectly, not constantly, but consistently and increasingly loving yourself no matter what is the most significant love story you'll live out. You don't have to find your beloved to become beloved. You just have to remember that you already are.

Today Is Enough

Lodro

Some months back I was with my friends at a bar and mentioned the new woman I'd been seeing. "Oh man," my friend Rodney said, "he's already in love with her. I can tell! You fall in love so much. You're probably in love with this table and we've only been here for twenty minutes."

"What can I say?" I replied. "It's a nice table."

As we engage in the practice of falling in love—with ourselves, with long-term partners, with platonic friends, and with lovers—we exercise our heart so that it can more fully accommodate all the vicissitudes life brings. Our heart is limitless in its capacity to love. We do not need objects for our love, such as a romantic partner (or as I joked, a table), in order to love fully. Sometimes you can just experience love.

The first step in learning to experience love at all times is to realize that you are basically whole. You do not need external circumstances to make you whole, be it a relationship, a degree, or a perfect job. You are already basically good. No one can rob you of that. This basic goodness is your innate state. You only need to wake up to your own indestructible nature.

Through the practice of meditation you learn that it is okay to look directly at yourself and experience that goodness acutely. You don't need to puff up who you are. You don't need to add anything on top of yourself. You don't need to hide any part of who you are. You can just manifest yourself fully. People will love you if you can be you. As Meggan stated earlier, loving yourself now, to the best of your ability, is cultivating what someone else will offer you in the future.

I was raised Buddhist, and have practiced meditation since I was 6 years old, but I went deeply with the practice on retreats starting at 17. The one thing I learned during this lifetime of studying Buddhism is that the Buddhist path begins and ends with your ability to let love flow. If you can discover that you are basically good, meaning that you are basically kind enough, capable enough, and worthy enough to love fully, then that is wonderful. But the discovery is just one aspect of your path. The rest of the path is developing true faith in your basic goodness. The more you develop trust in your innate state, the more you can love without hindrance.

One way to build that faith in your own goodness is to learn to be okay with being alone. Maybe you are single and live on your own and have a chance to practice being alone frequently. Even if you are romantically involved right now and stay with that person for the rest of your life you will still have times when you will be alone. Your partner will go away for work, or you will go on a vacation, or you may end up in a long-distance relationship for part of your time together. As Chögyam Trungpa Rinpoche stated, it is important to be okay with being alone, being "free-free." This is in stark difference to being "free-wild," where you fill up your life with activity after activity so you never have to glimpse your tender and vulnerable heart.

You can experience this sense of freedom anytime you are on your own. You don't have to cling to your smartphone or computer or even this book. You can take a moment to look up and say, *This is a wonderful opportunity I have. Right now, in this moment, I can befriend myself.* And then do it! Actually take the opportunity to offer yourself a sense of gentleness. We always have the space to befriend ourselves. There will be many times in our lives when we find ourselves alone. We can look to these times as fertile practice grounds for befriending and loving ourselves.

Having learned to love yourself and be okay with being alone, you are ready to offer that love to other people. Dating can be rough, and Meggan and I have shared some stories in that regard, but it's less so if you are willing to be openhearted with the people you are romantically interested in. In any given moment you have the option of dropping fixed expectations around what you think you need to be happy, who this other person is, and what your future together would be like. With fewer expectations, we can relax and discover who this being in front of us is.

Even if you have a long list of things you desire in a partner you may end up meeting someone who flies in the face of that list. So why bother limiting your love to someone with a certain hair color or profession? When you meet someone you can potentially offer your love to, explore that wholeheartedly.

This is the beginning of falling in love with another human being. It was all fun and games when we were on our own or testing the waters of being intimate with someone, but now there's a person who is our partner and invites us to offer our heart to them. How scary! But you can take the leap and fall in love, knowing the other person will fall right beside you. In that sense, falling in love is liberating. My friend Rodney was right about the woman I've been seeing, and, in fact, not one week after his statement she and I were flipping through a book of photos on my couch late one night when I turned to her and said, "Hi."

"Hi," she said, perking up.

"I've fallen in love with you," I said.

"Really?" she said, and paused, as my anxiety started to creep in. I took a breath.

She nuzzled against me and said, "I love you, too."

In that moment I knew I wasn't falling alone. There was someone who was willing to fall beside me, who was willing to meet discomfort by my side, ideally for quite some time. In a similar vein to what Meggan just said, it's not that this person is completing me; it's that she mirrors back my wholeness. We fall in love with another person not because we want to claim them, or own them in any way, but because we have found a partner who brings out the best in us.

The 14th-century meditation master Ngulchu Thogme wrote a text entitled *The 37 Practices of a*

Bodhisattva. The word *bodhi* is the same as in bodhicitta, meaning "open" or "awake." *Sattva* is "being" or "warrior." So a bodhisattva is a person who is willing to go to war against aggression by offering their heart fully. Ngulchu Thogme's text is full of teachings on how to live a life based in connecting with your own bodhicitta. In one of the passages he says:

> *When in reliance on someone your defects wane*
> *And your positive qualities grow like the waxing moon,*
> *To cherish such a spiritual friend more than your own body*
> *Is the practice of a Bodhisattva.*[3]

When you offer your love to another, it should not be because you need them. It should be because you cherish who they are, moment by moment, knowing that they will change (and so will you). It should be because your reliance on that individual has caused your defects and negative qualities to slowly fade away while your positive qualities are being cultivated rapidly.

Ngulchu Thogme was not talking about a romantic relationship, but there is no reason your partner cannot be your spiritual friend. Remember, in a true partnership this individual acts like a mirror, showing you those defects and positive qualities clearly so you can better grow as a person. Someone who is committed to growing spiritually while benefiting others is a bodhisattva, or openhearted warrior.

The openhearted warrior engages not just her or his lover with openness and compassion but all beings. You become a bodhisattva by expanding your heart to accommodate as many other people as possible—people who could benefit from your love! As discussed earlier, the path forward includes *maitri* (loving-kindness), *karuna* (compassion), *mudita* (sympathetic joy), and *up-eksha* (equanimity). As you cultivate these four qualities you expand your ability to open your heart beyond what you previously thought possible, to include people you like, those you don't like, and the millions of people you may never have even considered before.

It is a large task, but a bodhisattva is able to hold both heaven and earth. Here, *heaven* means the sky-high view of what is going on in a given situation, while *earth* is what needs to happen next. You can be walking down the aisle on your wedding day and considering what the rest of your life will look like with this person, for example. The earth aspect is the on-the-ground practicality of it all. You can hold the long-term view of your shared values and plans (heaven) but you also know you have to say your vows and thank everyone for coming today and that tomorrow one of you will need to unload the dishwasher (earth). Whether you love millions of people or just one in a given moment, you can join heaven and earth.

Joining heaven and earth can be uncomfortable, particularly when we are in a relationship with one person who we have vowed to cherish and be open with above all others. Thus the mark of a "good" relationship should not be how many times you say you love each other or how many years you spend in one another's arms but how you meet discomfort together. If you can remain present and openhearted with this ever-evolving person you have invited into your life then even when times get tough you can recommit to loving fully. A bodhisattva is able to hold the aspiration that their love can touch all beings, but on a day-to-day level see that their path comes down to remembering to smile at the person checking out their groceries at the supermarket.

The way to love no matter what is to be present enough to truly see that person checking out your groceries. The more you remain open to possibility and playfulness in your environment, the more opportunities you encounter to fall in love with others every day. Here I am talking about the great platonic loves of our lives. In the same way that I fell in love with Miranda and Gary and Meggan you have the chance (today!) to meet someone and develop a lifelong connection to them. These platonic loves are so valuable; whether you are in a romantic relationship or not, they will be there. To return to Ngulchu Thogme's advice, we should always cherish them as true spiritual friends.

Spiritual friends take many forms, and sometimes it may not be a long-term partner or a platonic love you are opening your heart to. Sometimes it may be a one-night stand, or a hook-up buddy, or someone you are just starting to date. Sex is an incredible way to offer love. But here's a reminder: Sex is dangerous territory. Sex without love can lead to people getting hurt, so it is important to always look at your intentions before leaping into bed with someone.

Having contemplated your intentions, though, you can create safe environments for the act itself, being present and in your own body, and at the end reflect on whether you feel uplifted or downtrodden. If the latter, don't beat yourself up; mistakes are part of our path and allow us to learn what we should never do again. If the former, however, then you likely used this intimate time with another person to engage in sacred sex. Sacred sex is just one of many ways to show love.

The act of loving others can take many forms, but the love itself is not bound in any way. We can love someone for a day, a month, a year, or a lifetime. And when that person leaves us, that love does not go away. There are many ways our loved one may depart from us. It can be a breakup, or divorce, or even death. No matter how it happens it can be devastating. We put our love in the form of another and then that other being disappeared. Just because that person is no longer with us does not mean the love disappears, too. There is simply a person-size hole where our love used to be. That love is now free to become more fluid, unconfined by that other person.

That disappearance can be shocking, but we heal with time. As Thich Nhat Hanh wrote, "Everything is impermanent. This moment passes. That person walks away. Happiness is still possible."[4] When you lose the one you love you can choose to drop the story line around the loss and just be with whatever you are feeling. By diving into the heart of what you feel, you explore it, learn from it, and come out feeling refreshed by the experience.

This is certainly preferable to the alternative that many of us choose, which is to escape from the pain and discomfort of our loss through a myriad of distractions. If you can be present enough to say no to those escapes and instead be with what you are feeling, I guarantee your love will take on new shape and you will heal your heart much faster.

Your heart bounces back because we all want to love. Love abounds. It is always available to us. We are innately loving, and innately lovable. That is the beautiful thing about being basically good. We have an unlimited ability to love. We must always begin and end with loving ourselves. People may come and go in our lives, and that is so incredible. We should cherish every minute they are here with us, that they love us and allow us to express our love to them. But they will go.

The fact that they will go is part of the natural cycle of relationships, romantic or otherwise. That is why Meggan and I did not want to write a book about finding everlasting happiness in another person, that one true love that if you can just discover then you will forever feel bliss. The idea of loving no matter what is that you are not constrained to offering your love to just one person. Because that person is not always going to be around (and that's okay).

We are all subject to the same aspects of life: change, impermanence, and death. I hate to drop the seemingly negative Buddhist stuff at the end, but as His Holiness the Karmapa once wrote, "Even with all of our intelligence, somehow we often do not consider the fact that friendships and partnerships will all eventually come to an end, either with the death of one member or with a voluntary separation."[5] We have to remember that loving fully means watching our love shift over time.

We change, moment by moment. You are not the same person you were years ago, and years from now you will look back at this time in your life and shake your head, remembering how different it was. Everyone else in your life also changes. That is a basic truth.

While love is infinite and boundless, the objects of our love are impermanent. You have likely had people come into your life, fallen in love with them, and had them leave. The relationship shifted. Either you were friends and then became lovers, or you were lovers who became friends. Or you entered one another's lives, had a torrid and brilliant love affair, and now you have no clue where they are anymore. This is the impermanent nature of relationships with others.

Finally, there is death. Even if we find *the* perfect person for us and we work very hard on our relationship, continuing to show up and meet discomfort together day after day for decades, at some point one of us will die. It is sad but true. Often in Buddhism we contemplate change, impermanence, and death not because we want to get depressed but because it reminds us to cherish the time we do have alive. We do not know when our partner will leave us. We do not know when we will die. We could die decades from now or be hit by a bus tomorrow. No matter what, we can love today.

That is my request of you: Please love today. Love yourself, for you are basically good enough and capable enough to do whatever you want to do. Develop faith in your worthiness of love. And share your heart with whomever you encounter. We have today to do it, and that is more than enough.

AFTERWORD

Meggan & Lodro

When we sat down with our wonderful, amazing editor and told her what specifically we were thinking of writing, she saw the vision for this book, and for that we are thankful. "One thing, though," she said. "By the end of this process you two are going to be in relationships." We scoffed.

"That's not the point," we chided. "The point is that love exists and that you can love yourself. You don't need another person in order to love."

And yet here we both are, hopelessly in love with sexy, vibrant, brilliant beings. Will things shift in our relationships? Indubitably. But regardless of whether either of our versions of "my David" is around by the time you read this sentence, the love that exists will have been nourishing and a potent reminder of what our hearts are capable of. By turning our minds more fully to love during the writing of this book and through the engagement in these practices, we have learned to love ourselves more and brought new people into our lives to share in that love. We hope the same for you.

So often people feel that our quest to be more spiritual, to be more connected to a sense of truth, to tranquility, or to the divine, has to be a solitary adventure. There's being pious or super monklike, and then on the other hand there's being in a relationship. We see one as blissed-out and serene, and the other as fairly chaotic.

But maybe the time has come to move the meditation cushion into the bedroom. Maybe it's time to wed our spiritual practice to our very human attempts at finding a real, embodied love with another. The effort of daring to really love someone else might be the only way to truly challenge and strengthen our capacity to connect to the divine or find equanimity within. Of course we can see Krishna on a mountaintop, the Buddha in a silent meditation hall, and the Goddess while on pilgrimage to the Isis temples of Egypt. But can we meet with what's most sacred while also being engaged in our day-to-day lives—while dating, while falling in love, while meeting with all those hidden or hard to see sides of ourselves that only someone else's love can reveal?

Yes. Armed with immense self-love, a Scooby gang of mystical-minded friends, and a spiritual arsenal of meditation practices and mantras, we believe it's not only possible but ideal. Figuratively bringing your mala beads or meditation cushions with you into your next relationship allows you to remain loyal to what's true for you. And most importantly it allows you to anchor deeply into the sources of love and self-worth that exist within you. Then you can tread a bit more lightly through the dating landscape knowing that your source of love doesn't depend on anyone external to you. It allows you to take more risks and have more fun, because your journey isn't about finding someone to love (which can be a stressful and painful waiting game); your journey is about finding someone to join you in the effort of loving yourself.

Merging our spiritual path with our romantic relationship ultimately allows us to have such a well-loved self that we can move beyond it. Having a partner who sees us, both the sculpted-bust version and the utter hot mess, lets us move past focusing on our own needs and desires and lets us get down to the tremendously fulfilling task of being a presence of love in the service of others.

ENDNOTES

Chapter 1

1. Marion Woodman, *Conscious Femininity: Interviews with Marion Woodman* (Toronto: Inner City Books, 1993), 81.

2. Hal Taussig, ed., "The Thunder: Perfect Mind," in *A New New Testament: A Bible for the Twenty-First Century* (New York: Houghton Mifflin Harcourt, 2013), 185.

3. Sakyong Mipham, *Ruling Your World: Ancient Strategies for Modern Life* (New York: Morgan Road Books, 2006), 101.

4. Pema Chödrön, *Living Beautifully with Uncertainty and Change* (Boston: Shambhala Publications, 2013), 50.

Chapter 2

1. Pema Chödrön, *The Places that Scare You: A Guide to Fearlessness in Difficult Times* (Boston: Shambhala Publications, 2001), 23.

2. Raymond Chandler, *The Long Goodbye* (New York: Vintage Crime/Black Lizard, 1992), 23.

3. Chögyam Trungpa, *Work, Sex, Money: Real Life on the Path of Mindfulness* (Boston: Shambhala Publications, 2011), 126.

4. Ibid., 119.

5. Karen King, *The Gospel of Mary of Magdala: Jesus and the First Woman Apostle* (Santa Rosa: Polebridge Press, 2003), 14–15.

Chapter 3

1. Ibid., 14.

2. Rainer Maria Rilke, *Rilke on Love and Other Difficulties*, trans. John J. L. Mood (New York: W. W. Norton, 1975), 98.

3. Ibid.

Chapter 4

1. Thich Nhat Hanh, *Fidelity: How to Create a Loving Relationship that Lasts* (Berkeley: Parallax Press, 2011), 55.

2. Ibid., 10.

3. Ibid., 81.

4. The Karmapa, Ogyen Trinley Dorje, *The Heart Is Noble: Changing the World from the Inside Out* (Boston: Shambhala Publications, 2013), 26.

5. Osho, *Being in Love: How to Love with Awareness and Relate Without Fear* (New York: Harmony Books, 2008), 197.

6. Ibid.

Chapter 5

1. King, *The Gospel of Mary of Magdala*, 16.

2. Esther Perel, *Mating in Captivity: Unlocking Erotic Intelligence* (New York: HarperCollins Publishers, 2006), 37.

3. Coleman Barks, *Rumi: The Big Red Book* (New York: HarperCollins Publishers, 2010), 377.

4. Robert Holden, Ph.D., *Loveability: Knowing How to Love and Be Loved* (New York: Hay House, 2013), 49.

5. Ibid., 51.

6. Hanh, *Fidelity*, 93.

7. Ibid.

8. Dorje, *The Heart Is Noble*, 24.

9. Hanh, *Fidelity*, 103.

Chapter 6

1. Dorje, *The Heart Is Noble*, 25.

2. Sakyong Mipham Rinpoche, *Turning the Mind into an Ally* (New York: Riverhead Books, 2003), 6.

3. King, *The Gospel of Mary of Magdala*, 15–16.

Chapter 7

1. William Blake, *The Marriage of Heaven and Hell* (Oxford: Oxford University Press, 1975), xvi.

2. Helen Schucman. *A Course in Miracles* (Mill Valley: Foundation for Inner Peace, 2007), Text–26. IX. 6–1.

3. King, *The Gospel of Mary of Magdala*, 15–16.

4. The papyrus manuscript of the Gospel of Mary was found over a hundred years ago. The first version, in Coptic, was discovered at Akhmim, and the next, in Greek, at Oxyrhynchus along the Nile in Egypt. The German scholar Dr. Carl Reinhardt, who found the manuscript at Akhmim (along with the Sophia of Jesus Christ, the Apocryphon of John, and the Act of Peter), believes that the passages that are missing in the Gospel of Mary were too incendiary even perhaps to the spiritual communities who sought to preserve it. In both versions, the first six pages are missing and then the three pages right after this quote. For more information, see the introduction to Dr. Karen King's *The Gospel of Mary of Magdala: Jesus and the First Woman Apostle*, 3–12.

5. "It is neither through the soul nor the spirit, but the nous between the two which sees the vision, and it is this which..." *The Gospel of Mary Magdalene*, trans. Jean-Yves Leloup (Rochester, VT: Inner Traditions, 2002), 31.

6. Tomas Spidlik, *The Spirituality of the Christian East*, trans. Anthony P. Gythiel (Kalamazoo: Cistercian Publications Inc, 1986), 332.

7. Ibid., 105.

8. Ibid., 333.

9. Ibid., 106.

10. Ibid.

11. Trungpa, *Work, Sex, Money*, 104.

Chapter 8

1. Chödrön, *The Places that Scare You*, 4.

2. I have Gwyneth Paltrow to thank for this term. I came across it while reading an article in *People* magazine from March 2014. She described her divorce with Coldplay lead singer Chris Martin as a "conscious uncoupling."

3. Murray Stein, *Transformation: Emergence of the Self* (College Station: Texas A&M University Press, 1998), 103.

4. Ibid., 101.

Chapter 9

1. Hal Taussig, ed., *A New New Testament: A Bible for the 21st Century Combining Traditional and Newly Discovered Texts* (New York: Houghton Mifflin Harcourt, 2013), 214.

2. Holden, *Loveability*, 27.

3. Ngulchu Thogme, *The 37 Practices of a Bodhisattva* (Ashland, OR: Marpa Foundation, 2001), Practice 6.

4. Hanh, *Fidelity*, 25.

5. Dorje, *The Heart Is Noble*, 29.

ACKNOWLEDGMENTS

From Lodro

I have loved many beings in my short life, and this book would not be here without you. You know who you are.

I would like to offer a special thank you to Brett Eggleston, David Delcourt, Rodney Solomon, Oliver Tassinari, Matt Bonoccorso, Jeff Grow, Will Conkling, Marina Acosta, Sara Bercholz, Milo Delcourt, Becca Abbott, Ethan Nichtern, Ellie Burrows, Laura Sinkman, Ericka Phillips, Susan Piver, Liz and Noah Isaacs, Anna Ruch, Dev Aujla, Heidi Sieck, Sarah Gokhale, and the UsGuys. Thank you to my parents, Beth and Carl, and siblings (and sibling-in-law), Michael, Jane, and Marcus, who have been pivotal models of love. Thank you to Adreanna Limbach for meeting discomfort with me, day in and day out. Thank you to Sakyong Mipham Rinpoche for his unwavering, loving presence.

You have all taught me more about love than I can possibly express in words. My hope is that I have channeled a fraction of your teachings into the pages of this book.

My heart fills with gratitude for Stephanie Tade, Patty Gift, and Sally Mason for seeing this book into completion, and the entire Hay House staff for your support.

From Meggan

I want to thank all things holy for giving me the opportunity to write this book. The divine pressure it took to create it has left me with a diamond. My own worth and love are now crystallized inside me.

It's an honor to get to love so many people in my life. Each is a teacher of mine. I'm especially grateful to my miraculous son, Shai Watterson Masi. He's a Jedi master when it comes to embodying true love.

I'm also grateful to my loving family in all of its traditional and nontraditional forms; to my co-parent, Joseph Nicholas Masi; and to all the loved ones no longer in my life, I'm more because of what we shared. Thank you.

To the ladyloves and sacred men in my life, you let me love courageously. I get to feel what the alchemists mean by gold. I know true wealth because of you: Danielle LaPorte, Kyle Gray, Kate Northrup Watts, Mike Watts, Gabrielle Bernstein, Paul William Morris, Alisa Vitti, Donna Freitas, Dr. Robert Holden, Rochelle Schieck, Dr. Deb Kern, Danielle Vieth, Latham Thomas, and Priya Tjerandsen.

I am deeply inspired by the spiritual legacy of Mary Magdalene. I have immense gratitude for what I have learned from her ministry, and for what she continues to reveal to me of a love that is both human and divine.

To Tracy Brown, I'm grateful for your unfaltering support. To Sally Mason, and all of my Hay House family, you've made the process seamless. And to the luminous Patty Gift, thank you for daring us to live this book.

I recently learned that the name David means beloved. And I felt humbled by the beauty and mystery of what happens when you follow your soul. Thank you, David Michael Odorisio, for being beloved to me.

ABOUTTHEAUTHORS

Lodro Rinzler is a teacher in the Shambhala Buddhist lineage and the author of five books on meditation, including the best-selling *The Buddha Walks into a Bar . . .* and the award-winning *Walk Like a Buddha.* Over the last 15 years he has taught numerous workshops at meditation centers, businesses, and college campuses throughout North America. Lodro's columns appear regularly in *The Huffington Post, Marie Claire,* and *Elephant Journal,* and he has been featured on WNYC, WBUR, FOX, the CBC, *Bloomberg Businessweek,* and *Fast Company.* He is the founder of the Institute for Compassionate Leadership, an authentic leadership training organization, and lives in Brooklyn with his dog, Tillie, and his cat, Justin Bieber. Website: www.lodrorinzler.com

Meggan Watterson is an author, international speaker, and Harvard-trained scholar of the divine feminine who inspires seekers to live from the audacity and authenticity of the voice of their soul. Her first book with Hay House, titled *REVEAL: A Sacred Manual for Getting Spiritually Naked,* is described as "ignited prayer" by Eve Ensler, "life-changing" by Dr. Christiane Northrup, and "a blessing to the world" by Gabrielle Bernstein. She has a master's of theological studies from Harvard Divinity School and a master's of divinity from Union Theological Seminary at Columbia University. She lives with her young son and his imaginary goose, Goldie. Website: www.megganwatterson.com

NOTES

NOTES

NOTES

N♡TES

Hay House Titles of Related Interest

YOU CAN HEAL YOUR LIFE, the movie,
starring Louise Hay & Friends
(available as an online streaming video)
www.hayhouse.com/louise-movie

THE SHIFT, the movie,
starring Dr. Wayne W. Dyer
(available as an online streaming video)
www.hayhouse.com/the-shift-movie

∽

DAILY LOVE: Growing into Grace, by Mastin Kipp

LIFE LOVES YOU: 7 Spiritual Practices to Heal Your Life,
by Louise Hay and Robert Holden

LOVEABILITY: Knowing How to Love and Be Loved,
by Robert Holden, Ph.D.

LOVE YOUR ENEMIES: How to Break the Anger Habit and Be a
Whole Lot Happier, by Sharon Salzberg and Robert Thurman

MIRACLES NOW: 108 Life-Changing Tools for Less Stress, More
Flow, and Finding Your True Purpose, by Gabrielle Bernstein

All of the above are available at your local bookstore,
or may be ordered by contacting Hay House (see next page).

∽

We hope you enjoyed this Hay House book. If you'd like to receive our online catalog featuring additional information on Hay House books and products, or if you'd like to find out more about the Hay Foundation, please contact:

HAY
HOUSE

Hay House, Inc., P.O. Box 5100, Carlsbad, CA 92018-5100
(760) 431-7695 or (800) 654-5126
(760) 431-6948 (fax) or (800) 650-5115 (fax)
www.hayhouse.com® • www.hayfoundation.org

———

Published in Australia by: Hay House Australia Pty. Ltd.,
18/36 Ralph St., Alexandria NSW 2015
Phone: 612-9669-4299 • *Fax:* 612-9669-4144
www.hayhouse.com.au

Published in the United Kingdom by: Hay House UK, Ltd.,
The Sixth Floor, Watson House, 54 Baker Street, London W1U 7BU
Phone: +44 (0)20 3927 7290 • *Fax:* +44 (0)20 3927 7291
www.hayhouse.co.uk

Published in India by: Hay House Publishers India,
Muskaan Complex, Plot No. 3, B-2, Vasant Kunj, New Delhi 110 070
Phone: 91-11-4176-1620 • *Fax:* 91-11-4176-1630
www.hayhouse.co.in

———

Access New Knowledge.
Anytime. Anywhere.

Learn and evolve at your own pace
with the world's leading experts.

www.hayhouseU.com

Printed in the United States
by Baker & Taylor Publisher Services